science fair

OCT -- 2002

Fish Tank Physics Projects

Madeline Goodstein

Enslow Publishers, Inc.

40 Industrial Road	PO Box 38
Box 398	Aldershot
Berkeley Heights, NJ 07922	Hants GU12 6BP
USA	UK

http://www.enslow.com

Dedication

In memory of a dear friend,
Lawrence Kershnar,
Who sparked so many novel ideas and,
many years ago, gave me the idea for this book.

Library of Congress Cataloging-in-Publication Data

Goodstein, Madeline
    Fish tank physics projects / Madeline Goodstein.
        p. cm. — (Science fair success)
    Includes bibliographical references and index.
    ISBN 0-7660-1624-2
    1. Optics—Experiments—Juvenile literature. 2. Liquids—Experiments—Juvenile
literature. [1. Optics—Experiments. 2. Light—Experiments. 3. Liquids—Experiments.
4. Experiments. 5. Science projects.] I. Title. II. Series.
    QC360 .G66 2002
    532'.0078—dc21

                      2001001380

Printed in the United States of America

10 9 8 7 6 5 4 3 2 1

To Our Readers:
We have done our best to make sure all Internet addresses in this book were active and appropriate
when we went to press. However, the author and the publisher have no control over and assume
no liability for the material available on those Internet sites or on other Web sites they may link
to. Any comments or suggestions can be sent by e-mail to comments@enslow.com or to the
address on the back cover.

Illustration Credits: Stephen F. Delisle

Cover Photo: Miracle Beam Marketing, Inc.

Contents

Introduction

What can you see when you look into an operating fish tank? Beautiful fish, special decorative pottery, sand, maybe seaweed and a tube that bubbles air. Surely, a fish tank is already a fascinating object as evidenced by the many aquariums that can be found in homes and offices. Yet a fish tank can be even more than that. It can be a striking, easy-to-use device for carrying out scientific experiments. A fish tank can be a window into the world of water science and of how nature works, a physics laboratory where you can easily observe unusual scientific effects as well as strange illusions. In this book, you are invited to observe these fascinating effects and illusions and to discover for yourself how they work.

In addition to the many experiments and discussions of principles involved, the book also contains numerous sections entitled "Project Ideas and Further Investigations." You can build upon any of the ideas in these sections to create your own original science fair project. Or, you may get an idea for another interesting experiment after you have completed one of those in the book. Bring your idea and plan to a teacher or other adult for review, and then start your own exploration.

Fish Tanks and Containers

You will need a five-gallon or a ten-gallon fish tank for the experiments in this book. A smaller tank or even a transparent plastic shoe box can instead be used for many of the experiments but usually, the bigger the tank, the more striking the effect. The most useful container will be large, transparent, rectangular, and squared at the corners. If your school has an aquarium, perhaps you would be allowed to use it for these experiments.

The tank needs a sturdy support when filled. A gallon of water weighs over eight pounds, so five gallons weigh over forty pounds. Ten gallons weigh more than eighty pounds. When you add in the weight of the tank itself, which may be up to twelve pounds, you will be dealing with almost one hundred pounds. The larger the tank, the heavier it is and the stronger the support that is needed. For this reason, it is never a good idea to move the tank while it is filled. The joints on the sides and bottom of the tank may buckle from the weight. A siphon, as will be explained later, can be used to easily empty water from the tank into a pail or sink.

Most of the experiments in this book may be carried out whether or not there are fish in the tank. Some experiments work even better in an operating fish tank. When fish are present, be careful to put the required materials into the tank without splashing or touching the fish. Too many decorative objects in the tank may interfere with your observations.

For the experiments in this book, the fish tank should be filled to within one to two inches of the top.

Scientific Method

All scientific experiments start with the question, "What if . . . ?" What if a ruler is lowered partway into water? Will the part under water look different than it did before? What if a glass is lowered bottom side up into water? Will the water fill the glass? The answer to a what-if question is found by carrying out an experiment. The question is usually called the problem.

Each scientific experiment deals with two variables. A variable is a property that can change. When one variable changes, the experiment reveals what happens to the other one. For example, the length of the ruler under water and the appearance of the ruler under water are variables. You can change the length under water and observe the change in appearance. The variable that you allow to change—in this case the length of the ruler in the water—is called the independent variable. The variable that changes as a result—in this case the appearance of the ruler under water—is called the dependent variable. Usually, no more than one independent variable can be allowed to change at a time in a scientific experiment. Otherwise, it is hard to tell which independent variable caused the change. For example, if you were to lower the ruler into the water and heat the water at the same time, you would not be able to tell which action produced the change observed in the appearance of the ruler.

When you plan an experiment, try to anticipate what will happen. In the case of the ruler, you might guess that the part under water will look shorter, or maybe longer, or perhaps wider or thinner. Your guess, based upon your own past experience, is called a hypothesis. The experiment will prove or disprove your hypothesis. If your hypothesis is disproved, that doesn't mean that the experiment wasn't scientific. All evidence obtained by experiment is important whether or not it supports the hypothesis.

After the experiment is concluded, try to explain the outcome. Perhaps different experiments are needed to improve the explanation. Good scientific experiments are productive in that they lead to new experiments and/or to new ideas.

Each topic in this book will be studied through a series of intriguing experiments designed to advance understanding of the physics involved. The fish tank will become a place to see and to appreciate the wonders of science.

Chapter 1

Light Refraction in a Fish Tank

Why do faceted diamonds and cut-glass goblets sparkle with such brilliance? Why do your feet seem closer than they really are when you stand in a tub of water? Why does a fishing rod appear to bend when thrust into water at a shallow angle?

The answer to all three questions is refraction. Refraction is the bending of a beam of light as it passes from one transparent material to another. Have you every seen a beam of light bend? Think of a flashlight beam. It may spread out, but it doesn't take a bend in midair. How about a searchlight shining up into the sky? It doesn't bend, either. Our everyday experience with light suggests that light always travels in straight lines. And indeed it does—except when it passes between two different transparent materials, as you shall see.

The illusions in which your feet appear closer than they are and in which a rod bends in water are just a few of those caused by refraction. The following experiments will first demonstrate some surprising illusions that you can see in a fish tank of water. Then you will carry out experiments to help explain why and how these illusions occur.

Experiment 1.1

Can You Believe Your Eyes?

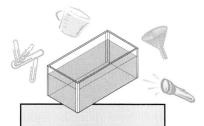

Materials

* fish tank or any large rectangular transparent container filled with water

* pencil

* your finger

* paper clip or coin

* ruler

Look through one of the sides of a fish tank filled with water. Your eyes should be slightly above the surface of the water. Holding that position, insert a pencil partway into the water in the tank. Observe what the pencil looks like when it is right in front of you. Then, tilt the pencil to the right. Keep your head in the same position and gradually move the pencil at the same angle all the way to the right. What appears to happen to the pencil? Next, move the tilted pencil back to the center and then slowly to the far left. What happens to the pencil? Remove the pencil from the water.

Insert one finger partway into the water. Move your head slowly right and then left. What appears to happen to your finger?

When the pencil is centered in the water, it looks much the same as before, except that it seems a little thicker below the water. When the tilted pencil is moved to the right, it appears to break into two parts that separate sideways from each other (see Figure 1). Then, when you move the pencil to the other side, the two parts of the pencil first move back together again and then appear to break apart in the other direction.

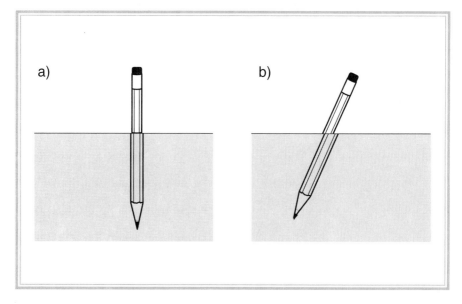

Figure 1. View when looking through the side of the fish tank at a pencil partially immersed in water. a) Pencil is vertical. b) Pencil is tilted.

When you put your finger into the water, you see it separate into two parts. You know that neither the pencil nor your finger is broken. These are visual illusions.

Try the following to see more visual illusions. For this part of the experiment, it is best if the tank does not contain fish that are large enough to try to swallow the paper clip or coin.

Drop or place a small flat object, such as a paper clip or coin, into the tank. The object should lie flat on the bottom about 1 to 2 inches away (3 to 5 cm) from one of the sides. The illusion will be visible even if there is gravel in the tank, as long as the gravel is level. From directly overhead, look down at the object in the water. While in this position, point to the spot on the side of the tank that appears to be level with the object. Keep your finger in place and look at the object through the side of the tank. Is the object where your finger is pointing? Remove the object from the water.

Lower a ruler vertically into the tank while you observe it directly in front of you from a little above the water surface. When one inch of ruler has been lowered into the water, compare the approximate length below the water with one inch of the ruler above the water. Lower two inches of the ruler into the water and compare the approximate length below the water with that of two inches of ruler above the water. Finally, lower the ruler into the water to its three-inch mark and compare the approximate length below water with three inches of the ruler above water.

When you pointed to the object that you had dropped to the bottom of the tank, did you find that you were actually pointing to a spot about two to three inches above the bottom? This is similar to the illusion mentioned before when you look at your feet in a filled tub or in a swimming pool.

When the ruler is moved into the water, it appears to shorten. The one-inch length appears to be about one-half inch. The ruler continues to appear to shorten as it is lowered deeper into the water. When raised back up out of the water, the ruler, of course, has not been shortened at all.

People have long known that objects in water can look as if they are somewhere other than where they actually are. Spear fishers have known this for eons. Arabian scientists were examining this phenomenon as long as 900 years ago. What causes these illusions? The major clue is that they always take place when light has to pass between water and air. The next experiments will look further into this.

Project Ideas and Further Investigations

- When you observe an object in water from the side, such as a spoon dipped partway into water, does the top half or the bottom half of the object move as you move your head? If you move farther away from the tank, is there a change in the effect?
- When a pencil is dipped into water, does the pencil appear to break or otherwise change when moved forward or back in the water? Investigate and explain.
- Observe an object dipped partway into water while you move your head first higher and then lower. Is there an optical illusion? If so, describe it. Does it make any difference how high or low above the water surface your head is?
- Observe and describe or make drawings showing the effect on objects of different shapes partially immersed in water when viewed from different angles. Look, for example, at a straw, pencil, small ball, can, etc.
  - Glue a coin to the bottom of a ruler. It represents a fish. How deep does the fish appear to be when it is immersed at different lengths in the water? Graph the actual height compared to the apparent height. Explain how someone fishing in a stream with a spear has to take this into consideration.

Experiment 1.2

When Do We See Light?

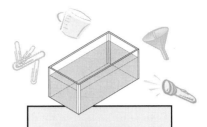

In order to understand why the visual illusions seen in Experiment 1.1 occur, it is important to know some of the properties of light.

Suppose you look at a fish tank in a totally darkened room. Are you able to see the tank? If you turn the light on, can you see it? Why is there a difference?

You can only see light that reaches your eyes. If a room has no light in it, you will not be able to see anything. When you turn the light on, the light will strike the objects

Materials

* fish tank or any large rectangular transparent container filled with water

* darkened room

* narrow-beam flashlight or flashlight with aluminum foil, scissors, large nail, and tape

* white or light-colored wall or white poster board with tape

* optional: long flat piece of Styrofoam

in the room and some of that light will be bounced over to your eyes. The light that is bounced back to your eyes is called reflected light. It is the light reflected to your eyes that makes the objects visible.

Does light travel in a straight line in air? To investigate this, use a flashlight that has a beam that does not spread out much. If your flashlight does not have a narrow beam, fix it in the following way:

Cut a piece of aluminum foil large enough to completely cover the bulb end of your flashlight. With a large nail, make a smooth hole in the center of the foil. Wrap the foil firmly around the flashlight so that the hole is right over the bulb. Tape or hold the foil in place.

To see how light travels through air, a dark room is needed. You can either pull down all the shades or do the experiment at night without light.

Find a plain wall that is white or light in color or use a piece of white poster board taped to the wall. Turn on the flashlight in the darkened room. Hold the flashlight horizontally and place the side of it flat against the wall. You should be able to see the beam of light shining forward against the wall. Is the beam of light straight or does it bend or curve?

The beam of light travels in a straight line through the air near the wall. It probably spreads out a bit. It neither bends nor curves.

The next question is whether light travels in a straight line through water. You can try shining your beam through the water in the fish tank. For this part of the experiment, having fish in the tank is an advantage. Usually, a tank with fish in it has plenty of floating dirt particles. The dirt particles will bounce the light over to your eyes so that you can easily see the beam.

If you cannot easily see the beam of light, your water is probably too clean. In that case, you can adapt the wall technique that was used for light in air. However, this time you will need a waterproof board. A long, clean Styrofoam tray from the meat or vegetable department at the supermarket can be used for this. Cut away the rounded sides to make a flat sheet. Now you have a waterproof board. You can shine a light beam along the board by holding the side of the flashlight against it.

Lower the Styrofoam board vertically so that it is partway into the water in the fish tank. Hold the flashlight vertically above the tank of water. Shine the beam straight down against the Styrofoam board through the water. Then, shine it against the board from one side of the tank to the other. Does light move in a straight line in water?

According to the above experiments, light moves in a straight line both while in the air and while in the water.

Experiment 1. 3

Refraction

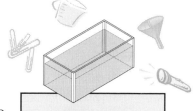

What happens to a light beam to cause visual illusions when it passes between air and water? This experiment will investigate what happens when the angle that the entering light makes to the water surface is gradually changed. As in Experiment 1.2, a Styrofoam board will be used to make the beam visible in both air and water.

Materials

❊ fish tank or any large rectangular transparent container filled with water

❊ Styrofoam board

❊ darkened room

❊ narrow-beam flashlight

Lower a Styrofoam board vertically so that about half of it is in the water in the fish tank (see Figure 2). Darken the room. Shine the beam of light from above the tank along the side of the board into the water at an angle only slightly above the horizontal. You should be able to see the beam in the air and in the water. Observe the path of the beam. Next, gradually increase the angle to the water surface at which you shine the beam. Each time, observe the path of the beam from air into water. Finally, observe the beam as you shine it vertically into the water.

Did you see the light beam bend as it entered the water? Which way did it bend? How does the angle of the bend change as the beam moves from horizontal to vertical?

As a light beam enters water from air at an angle to the surface, the beam bends downward. The bend in the light beam is greatest when the beam is closest to horizontal. The bend becomes smaller as the beam becomes more vertical. A fully vertical beam moves straight down without bending.

The change in direction of a beam of light as it passes from one transparent material to another is called refraction.

Light is refracted because it changes speed as it passes from one transparent material to another. Light slows when it passes from air into water. The part that enters the water first slows down first. As more of the beam enters, it slows down, too. The successive slowing causes light entering at an angle to change direction. It bends downward.

Refraction can be compared to a speeding car moving at an angle from pavement to sand. One front wheel reaches the sand first and slows. The other wheel continues spinning as before. The car swivels toward the sand because it is being

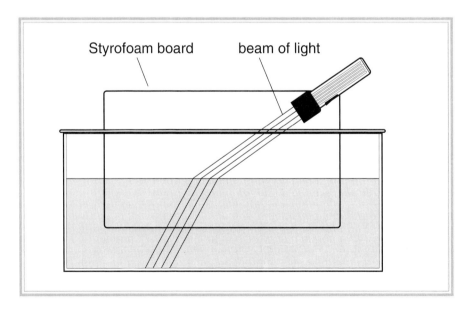

Figure 2. A beam of light enters the fish tank, from air into water, at an angle. The beam is shining against a Styrofoam board held vertically halfway into the water.

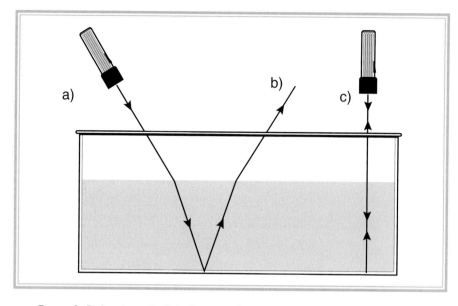

Figure 3. Refraction of a light beam is shown going between air and water. a) A light beam is bent as it enters the water at an angle to the surface. b) A reflected beam is bent at the reverse angle as it exits from water into air. c) The light beam enters the water vertically and is reflected upward vertically.

pushed faster on one side. It keeps turning until both front wheels are in the sand. Then it continues in the new direction.

A beam of light that enters the water vertically does not bend. This is because all of the beam enters the water together and is slowed down together.

When a beam exits from water into air, the beam speeds up. The reverse bending occurs as it exits from the water. This causes refraction in the opposite direction. See Figure 3.

Project Ideas and Further Investigations

- Make a multiple-exposure photograph or a drawing to show the observations of what happens when light beams enter from air into water at greater and greater angles.
- Does the length through which the beam passes in air make a difference as to how much the beam is bent on entering the water? What is your hypothesis about this? Conduct experiments to find out.
- What happens to a beam of light that passes from water into air at different angles to the surface? If your fish tank has a transparent bottom, you can shine a beam upward into the water and record what happens when it travels on into the air. If not, you can enclose a narrow-beam flashlight in a plastic bag and seal it so that no water can get into the bag. Arrange the plastic so that a thin beam can be aimed upward from the water through the surface. Draw diagrams or take photographs of how the beam looks in the water and air when aimed at several different angles to the surface.
- Is light refracted as it passes through a pane of glass? Glass slows light a little more than water does. Find out what happens by doing experiments. Explain your observations.

Experiment 1.4

The Eye Fools
the Brain

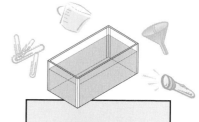

What causes us to see all these strange illusions just because the light bends? The reason has to do with our brains. When a ray of light reaches the eye, the brain assumes that the ray has moved from the object to the eye in a straight line. It does not recognize that the light has been bent. The

Materials

* fish tank or any large rectangular transparent container filled with water

* thread

* small object such as a stone or paper clip

* small stick

result is that we see the object in the wrong place.

To see how this assumption fools the brain, see Figure 4. In this drawing, a ray of light from the sun or some other source has been reflected from a fish in a fish tank. The reflected ray is bent (refracted) as it exits into the air. The viewer assumes the ray is unbent. As a result, the viewer thinks the fish is higher up than it actually is.

Observe this for yourself. Use thread to hang a small object from one end of a small stick. Look through the water at an angle from above while you place the object in various positions in the tank. Note where it appears to be each time. Check the actual position by viewing it from the side. Compare. Do your observations confirm the explanation above?

This same assumption by the brain that light travels in a straight line explains other illusions in this chapter, such as the pencil and finger that are not really broken.

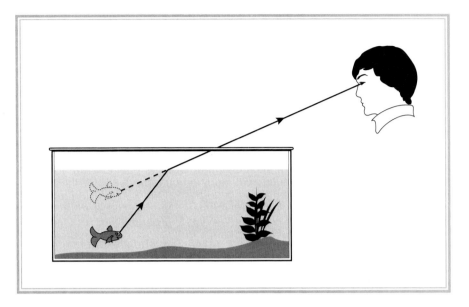

Figure 4. A light beam is reflected from the fish. As the beam exits from the water, it is refracted. The refracted beam reaches the viewer's eye. The dotted line is the line of sight that the viewer accepts as the real one. As a result, the fish looks closer to the surface than it actually is.

In Asia, there is an unusual fish called the archerfish. What makes it different is that it preys upon insects and spiders that are on twigs above the water in which it lurks. From below the target, the fish shoots up a powerful jet of water that knocks its dinner off the branch. How does the fish manage to aim its jet so accurately? How does it avoid the misleading effect of light refraction?

The answer is that the archerfish positions itself directly under the target. From that position, the light is moving at a 90-degree angle to the surface of the water. The light is not bent.

Project Ideas and Further Investigations

- Observe from different angles the effect on the image of transparent glass objects placed under water—such as a thick-walled jug, a sphere, and a stirring rod. Explain.
- Suppose a fish were looking upward at an angle through the water to a person looking into the tank. How would refraction affect the fish's view? Show by a diagram.
- Send a beam of light horizontally through the tank from outside of one side through the water and through the opposite side. Then, tilt the flashlight slightly downward and observe what happens to the beam in the tank and after it exits. Gradually increase the tilt, observing the beam throughout. Where and how does refraction occur? What effects does it cause? Make diagrams of these.
- What happens to the magnifying effect when you put a magnifying glass into water? Explain.
- How should a fisherman casting his lure into the water allow for the effect of refraction? Explain in words and with a diagram.
- From the side of a swimming pool, would you dive in front of or behind a coin to get it from the bottom? Explain in words and with a diagram. **Never experiment in a pool of water without adult supervision.**
  - Why can you see much better underwater with goggles than without goggles? How does the eye material and shape of a fish's eye accommodate the refraction due to water?

Experiment 1.5

Converting White Light into a Spectrum of Colors

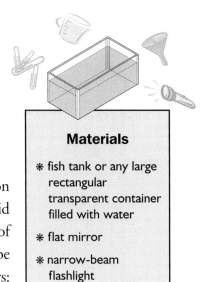

This experiment shows not an illusion but something very real. With the aid of a mirror, a flashlight, and a tank of water, it shows how white light can be separated into its component colors: the spectrum.

Materials

* fish tank or any large rectangular transparent container filled with water

* flat mirror

* narrow-beam flashlight

Hold a mirror completely within the water, facing upward at an angle. From above, shine a narrow beam of light onto the mirror, as shown in Figure 5.

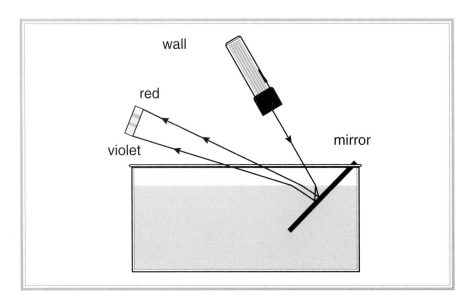

Figure 5. Reflected light from a mirror is refracted as it exits from water into air. Each color in the light is refracted at a different angle. An image of a spectrum appears on the wall.

Look for a spot of light appearing on the nearest wall. Gradually tilt the mirror until you see the spot on the wall burst into a lineup of colors. Note the order of the colors, starting from the left side.

You can also do this using bright sunlight instead of a flashlight. How do the colors compare to those produced by the flashlight?

White light is made up of many different colors. When you shine light from air into water and the mirror sends it back out again, each color in the beam of light is refracted a little differently from the others. The result is a spectrum. Violet light is bent the most and red the least.

Project Ideas and Further Investigations

- Obtain some transparent pieces of plastic, each of a different color. Each should be large enough to cover the front of the flashlight. Beam each color onto a mirror in the water and look for it on the wall. Which colored beam bends the most? Which bends the least? Arrange the colors in order from the greatest bend to the smallest.
- By shining the narrow beam of light through the fish tank in various directions, other shapes and variations of the spectrum will appear even without the mirror. Where do these occur? What colors are seen? Discuss and explain your results.
- Compare the spectrum produced when a mirror refracts light from water to the spectrum produced when a prism refracts light in air. Explain any differences.
- Compare the way a prism refracts light in air to form a spectrum to the way it refracts light in water. Explain any differences.

Chapter 2

Light Reflection in a Fish Tank

We can see the sun and the stars, fire, glowing light bulbs, and certain tiny luminous sea creatures simply because each is a light emitter. Each gives off light that beams to our eyes. How do we see the moon, streets, pictures, our homes, and everything else in our world that does not give off light? We see them by reflected light. Without their own light, most objects are visible to us only when beams of light strike it and are bounced back to our eyes. We see our own faces only when light that strikes us is then reflected to a mirror that reflects the beams back to our eyes. It may seem complicated, but it works very well.

In ancient times, before glass mirrors were developed, people could see their images only in a still pool of water or a polished metal surface. Greek mythology tells the story of Narcissus, who was so beautiful he fell in love with his own image in a small pool. Narcissus lay beside the water all day every day gazing at his reflection until he wasted away and died. On that spot, as the story tells, the beautiful flower that now bears his name sprang up.

Chapter 1 focused on refraction, the bending of a beam of light when it passes at an angle between two transparent materials. Both refraction and reflection are of great importance to our daily lives because they determine most of what we are able to see in our world.

A fish tank is an excellent tool to discover the laws that govern reflection and to find out how reflection and refraction interact.

Experiment 2.1

Windows and Mirrors

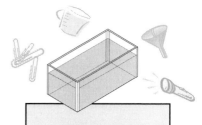

Materials

✻ fish tank or any large rectangular transparent container filled with water

✻ assorted objects placed outside the fish tank

✻ fork

✻ pencil

For the following experiment, it is best if the fish tank or container contains only water.

Position yourself so that you are looking through the water in the tank from the middle of one long side toward the opposite long side. Is the pane of glass on the opposite side transparent or is it acting as a mirror? Repeat looking through the two short sides.

Position yourself again so that you are looking through the water in the tank from the middle of one long side. Now look up toward the surface of the water. Do you see a mirror or are you looking through a transparent surface?

From the same position in front of a long side, look through the water to the adjacent short side. Is the adjacent side a window or a mirror? Try looking through each of the vertical glass sides to the adjacent side. You may wish to put an object into the water to help decide which pane is acting as a window and which as a mirror.

From above one side of the tank, look through the water toward each of the other sides of the tank. Can you see through the sides? Can you see objects outside the tank? Hold your finger outside the glass to see if it is visible. If you can't see through the side, what do you see?

Finally, if your tank has a glass bottom, look straight down at it from above. Is the surface of the water a window or a mirror? Is the bottom glass a window or a mirror?

Did you suspect in advance that the views into the tank would be so complicated? Did you suspect that some views would result in seeing mirrors rather than windows, and did you guess which ones they were?

The front and side panes of the fish tank act as windows when you look straight through them to the opposite side. The side panes become mirrors when you look at them through the water from above or from below at an angle. When you look from one pane through the water toward an adjacent pane, the front pane is transparent and the adjacent one is a mirror. The surface is transparent when you look straight down at it. It is a mirror when you look upward at it from one of the sides.

Visually, a fish tank is complex. Following are some demonstrations of other window/mirror effects in a fish tank.

Hold a fork by its handle. From one side of the tank, look up toward the surface of the water. Lower the fork vertically until the tines are halfway into the water. What do you observe? Remove the fork.

Position yourself so that you are looking through the water up toward one of the sides. Can you see through the side? Hold a pencil about an inch away from the outside of the glass on the side that you are viewing. Can you see the pencil through the fish tank? Hold the pencil flush against the glass. Can you see it now?

Look into the tank and find where several other surfaces act as mirrors. Can you find a clue to help explain what is happening?

As you move the fork into the water while looking up toward it, the tines lengthen until they have narrow sharp points at both the top and bottom. What you are seeing are the tines in the water and their reflection from the surface. The surface is transparent when you look down into it from above but becomes a mirror when you look up at it from one side.

When looking through the water from below the surface, a pencil outside the tank cannot be seen at all. The glass acts as a mirror and is not transparent to you.

Did you find any clue as to why these effects are seen? Here is one clue for you to consider. The panes are transparent whenever you look *straight through* them either vertically or horizontally. However, when you look through the water from one surface to another *at an angle to each other*, the second surface becomes a mirror. That is, you can look straight through the tank from one side to the other, or you can look straight through from top to bottom. Each time, the water and the panes are transparent. But, when you look up from one side through the water to the surface, or look from one side to an adjacent side, the shape of the fish tank forces you to look through the water at an angle. Each time, the second surface acts as a mirror.

The next experiments will investigate this further, but first it is necessary to consider the rules that govern reflection.

Project Ideas and Further Investigations

- Lower some objects, other than those viewed in Chapter 1, such as a spoon, ball, paper clip, or open end of a glass, partly into the water. Observe them while you look upward toward the water surface. Make a report on what you see.

- When the surface of the water acts as a mirror, is the image reversed? Is the image inverted? Test this out with a ruler. Describe any differences between the image and the original. How does it compare to that in an ordinary glass mirror (silvered glass)? Which gives a better reflection, an ordinary glass mirror or the fish tank? Explain.

- Diagram all the views in a fish tank. In addition to window and mirror effects, look for and include views that show refraction. For each, state whether the view from one surface to another is at an angle or straight through.

Experiment 2.2

Reflections from Water

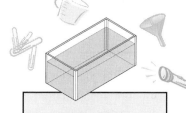

How is light reflected from water? How can water be transparent and reflecting? What rules govern the process? The fish tank can be used to help find answers.

Carry out this experiment at night or in a room with the windows covered. The room has to be dark for this experiment because only about 10 percent of a light beam is reflected from water.

Materials

* fish tank or any large rectangular transparent container filled with water
* darkened room
* narrow-beam flashlight
* index card

Shine a narrow-beam light from above into the water. You should be able to see both a refracted beam in the water and a reflected beam above it. Search the ceilings and walls in the room to find the reflected spot of light. Hold an index card in line with the beam to bring the spot closer to you. Observe the angle at which the beam is reflected.

Change the angle of the beam from the flashlight to the water. How does the angle of the reflected beam change? Make several additional changes to the angle of the approaching beam and compare each time to the angle of the reflected beam.

Compose a rule to describe how the angle of the approaching beam compares to the angle of the reflected beam.

As the beam of light reaches the water, it splits. Part is reflected up into the air. Part is refracted down in the water.

How does the angle at which the beam is reflected compare to the angle made going toward the water? *When a light beam shines at an angle toward a reflecting surface, the beam is reflected onward at the same angle that it made going toward the surface.* This is the law of reflection and it applies to any kind of reflection of light—from a shiny surface, from a wall, from water, from glass, from a mirror, or from any other surface. It applies whether the light is from a light source (such as the flashlight) or is reflected light from another surface.

To measure the approach angle, physicists make use of the normal line. The normal line is a line that is perpendicular to the surface. The approach angle is the angle between the light beam and the normal line where the beam strikes the surface. This angle can be used whether or not the surface is level. Similarly, the reflected angle is the angle between the reflected beam and the normal line to the surface. Figure 6 diagrams how a beam is reflected and refracted as it goes from air to water. The law of reflection says that the approach angle always equals the reflected angle.

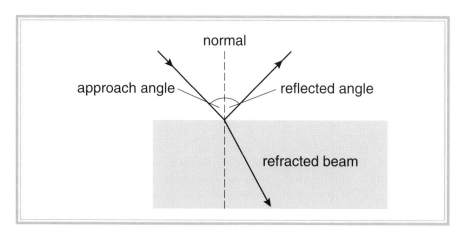

Figure 6. A light beam is reflected and refracted at the air/water interface.

Project Ideas and Further Investigations

• Compare an approach angle and its reflected angle for a beam of light going toward the surface of water by taking measurements of the angles. Repeat for several different approach angles. Do your measurements support the law of reflection?

• Are the approach and reflected angles equal for light beamed onto linseed oil, rubbing alcohol, or other liquids?

Experiment 2.3

Total Internal Reflection

The mirror behaviors in a fish tank are the result of total internal reflection. To see how this works, try the following experiment.

Shine a narrow beam directly upward through the water from the lower end of one side of the fish tank. The beam should be as close to

Materials
✳ fish tank or any large rectangular transparent container filled with water
✳ narrow-beam flashlight
✳ Styrofoam board, if needed

vertical as you can get it. You need to be able to see the beam both in the water and in the air. If you need to make the beam more visible, follow the directions for using the Styrofoam board in Experiment 1.3.

Next, tilt the beam a little downward from the vertical path. How is its path through the water and air affected? Continue tilting the beam farther from the vertical position. What happens?

Figure 7 shows what happens as a beam of light enters the water from below at different angles from the vertical. Initially the beam is refracted into the air. As the beam is tilted away from the vertical, a dim reflected beam begins to appear in the water. The angle of this dim reflected beam is equal to the approach angle. At the same time, the refracted beam is bent closer to the water.

The more the incident, or incoming, beam tilts away from the vertical, the more the refracted beam bends toward the

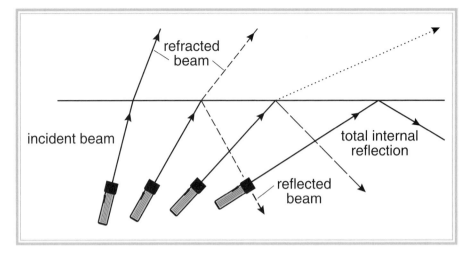

Figure 7. TOTAL INTERNAL REFLECTION AT THE WATER/AIR INTERFACE. This diagram shows what happens when a flashlight sends a beam upward through water into air. As the approach angle increases, the refracted ray becomes dimmer and the reflected light becomes brighter. When the approach angle becomes greater than the critical angle (48.6 degrees from the normal), the angle of refraction becomes greater than 90 degrees. All of the light is bent back toward the water. This is total internal reflection.

water and the dimmer it gets. Meanwhile, the reflected beam becomes brighter. Eventually the refracted beam will skim the surface of the water. When the angle of the light beam away from the vertical is increased any farther, the refracted light can no longer get out of the water. All of the light is reflected. The striking effect when all of the beam bounces back into the water is called total internal reflection.

Total internal reflection causes a transparent surface to become a mirror. Note that total internal reflection occurs when light speeds up as it starts to exit one material and enter into another. This means that total internal reflection can only take place when going from water into air, not in the reverse direction.

The angle to the normal at which total internal reflection occurs is called the critical angle. The critical angle depends upon the materials through which the beam moves. For water into air, the critical angle is 48.6 degrees; for any angle larger than 48.6 degrees, total internal reflection occurs.

A diamond's sparkle is due to one of the smallest critical angles of any transparent material, 24.4 degrees. Any beam at a larger angle to the normal line than 24.4 degrees is reflected back into the diamond. Diamonds are specially cut to reflect light brilliantly out to our eyes. To do this, the light undergoes several total internal reflections from each of the facets before it is bounced back through the top surface. Without such facets, the light would simply exit through the bottom of the diamond (see Figure 8).

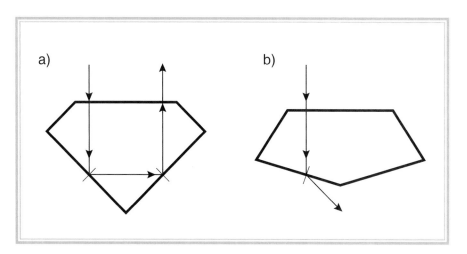

Figure 8. Maximum brilliance is produced by cutting the facets of a diamond to take advantage of its critical angle, 24.4 degrees. a) Sparkle is produced when light enters through the flat top facet and undergoes at least two total internal reflections before exiting. b) Brilliance is lost when light enters through the flat top facet and simply exits at the second boundary. It exits when the approach angle at the second boundary is less than the critical angle.

Project Ideas and Further Investigations

- An excellent demonstration of total internal reflection can be carried out in a fish tank using small mirrors two to three inches long. A strong, narrow-beam flashlight is needed. Prop up the small mirrors at different angles in a row at the bottom of one side of the tank. Oil-based clay is handy for propping up the mirrors. When a beam of light is sent straight down onto one of the angled mirrors, it will be reflected upward at an angle toward the surface. Arrange the mirrors so that the reflected beam is returned at a greater and greater angle from vertical. Observe how and when there is refraction out of the water, reflection into the water, and total internal reflection. Compare the intensities of the refracted and reflected beams. Take measurements of the angles. Make photographs or diagrams of what you observe.

- You can use the critical angle of water to predict when the surface in the fish tank will act as a mirror. For this project, select a specific size for the fish tank, such as five gallons. Assume that the tank is filled almost to the top. Show by diagrams from different viewpoints when the viewing angle is larger than the angle at which total internal reflection occurs. When the viewing angle is larger, the second surface viewed becomes a mirror. Measure the angles of approach and reflection and see if they verify the theory.

- When a narrow beam shines upward into the water in a fish tank that has glass sides and a glass bottom, a spot of light may be observed on the ceiling in the opposite direction to that of the refracted beam. This phenomenon is not ordinarily described in the introductory physics books. Look through physics books and other physics publications to see if you can find any reference to it. Formulate a hypothesis to explain this spot of light. Devise experiments as needed to test your hypothesis.

Experiment 2.4

How Many Spoons Are in the Tank?

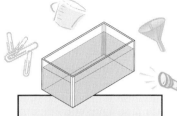

Here is one last optical illusion for a fish tank.

Face one corner of a fish tank at eye level. Hold a spoon by the handle above the water about one inch from the corner. Slowly lower the spoon vertically into the water until

it is halfway in while you observe it at eye level. How many spoons do you see in the water?

Still holding the spoon vertically in the water, slowly move it at the same height diagonally away from you toward the opposite corner. How many spoons do you see now and where are they?

Repeat moving the spoon away from the front corner, but this time notice where the top of the actual spoon is.

Initially, even though there was only one spoon in the tank, you probably saw two. The effect is really there—it can be photographed. If there are fish in the tank, look for the same effect as they swim by the corner.

As the two images move toward the other corner, they also move farther apart. Now five spoons can soon be seen in the water. We know that there is only one real spoon. The upper portion of the real spoon can be seen above the water surface between the images. Which are reflections and which are refractions?

Project Ideas and Further Investigations

- Any ordinary light that enters a fiber optic cable under-goes total internal reflection. The reflections continue onward so that a ray of light travels through the cable from one end to the other even when the cable is curved. Obtain a length of fiber optic cable and investigate the way light travels through it. How is this process used for long-distance communications and in medicine?

- Does the critical angle of a substance change with temperature? Make a prediction. Then conduct experiments to verify your prediction.

- Develop plans for an entertaining light show around an indoor or outdoor swimming pool by taking advantage of the reflection and refraction effects in the water. **With adult supervision**, test out each of the effects and modify as needed to make them even more striking. **Do not place any electrical device or wires leading to an electrical device so that it touches or could fall into the water**.

Chapter 3

Surface Tension

Why do falling leaves float on water rather than sink below the surface, and why do they sink once they are submerged? Why do drops of water sit separately in a rounded shape on a sheet of waxed paper rather than collapsing into a film of water on the paper? Why does rain fall in separate rounded drops? Why do soap bubbles close up as they are blown free of the ring? Surface tension, a property of all liquids, is responsible for these familiar behaviors. Surface tension causes a liquid to act as if it has a thin, slightly elastic film on its surface. All bodies of water—oceans, lakes, filled bathtubs, cups of water—behave as if this thin film were covering them.

Besides explaining certain effects that we see around us, surface tension is used by scientists to provide useful information during certain scientific investigations. Changes in surface tension, for example, indicate the effectiveness of detergents, the nature of foaming, the presence of other chemicals, and the progress of chemical reactions.

What causes surface tension, and what effects are due to it?

Experiment 3.1

Can a Needle Float?

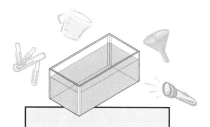

Would you believe that you can get a small needle to float on the surface of water even though it is made of steel? If your fish tank is operating with either fish or an aerator, it would be better to use another container for this experiment. A calm surface is needed for it.

Materials

* cup, bowl, fish tank or other container filled with water

* small needle

* fork

* thread

* large straight needle (such as a darning or embroidery needle)

Try to float a small needle on top of water in a container. It helps if you place the needle across the tines of a fork and use the fork to gently lower it to the water. Observe the surface of the water touching the needle. What is different about it? How can you cause the floating needle to sink? What holds the needle up?

Thread the same needle and lower it to the water with its point down. Can you get the needle to float on its point?

Obtain a large needle, such as a darning or embroidery needle. Can you get it to float? Why is there a difference between what happens with the small and the large needles?

It is the "skin" on the surface of the water due to surface tension that holds up the small needle. The weight of the needle stretches the elastic skin. You can see the surface curving downward around the needle. Although the surface tension of water is large compared to that of most other liquids, it is still only barely strong enough to hold up the small needle.

As with any elastic, the surface can be stretched only so far before it breaks. A small disturbance such as a ripple in the water is often enough to sink the needle.

When lowered point down into the water, the needle sinks. Since it has the same weight as before, why does it sink? The answer has to do with the pressure that the needle exerts on the water. Consider that the downward pressure exerted by an object depends on two things: how heavy the object is (how much downward force it exerts) and how big the area is on which its weight rests. If the area remains the same, then the heavier the object, the greater the pressure it exerts. On the other hand, if the force is kept the same, the smaller the area upon which it acts, the greater the pressure. If the same force is spread over a much larger area, then the pressure becomes much smaller.

In the case of the needle, the area of its point is much smaller than the area of its side. For the same downward force due to the weight of the needle, the pressure will be greater on the smaller area. The area of the side of the needle is much bigger, so the needle exerts much less downward pressure on any given area when it is on its side. That is why the needle can float on its side but crashes through the surface when on its point.

Why does a larger needle sink? A large needle does not have much more surface than a smaller one. However, it can weigh much more in comparison. The greater weight over an only slightly larger area results in greater pressure and the needle sinks.

A sharp knife easily cuts cheese or bread because the downward force acts on a very thin edge. If the edge is dull, it has a larger area, so more pressure is needed to get the knife to cut.

Liquids are made up of exceedingly tiny particles called molecules that tend to attract each other. The attraction of the identical molecules to each other in a liquid is called cohesion. Below the surface of a liquid, the cohesive attractions come from all around a molecule. The attractions are balanced so that a molecule isn't pulled in any one direction (see Figure 9a). However, up at the surface, things are different. The surface molecules are attracted by neighboring molecules on the sides and below, but there are no liquid molecules above to exert a balancing attraction. It is this imbalance of forces that creates surface tension. The uneven attractions pull the surface molecules inward and toward each other to form a network of molecules at the surface that acts as a film.

Water has an unusually high surface tension, which is due to its molecular composition. Each molecule of water has one oxygen atom linked to two hydrogen atoms. The two hydrogen atoms are attracted not only to their own oxygen atom but also to nearby oxygen atoms (see Figure 9b). As a result, all the molecules of water tend to be attracted to each other more strongly than is usual for other liquids.

Surface tension is what makes it possible for insects called water striders (or pond skaters) to run across the surface of a pond. These insects have six flattened feet that help to spread out their weight. The surface is a death trap for insects that fall into the water near water striders. Trapped beneath the surface skin, the insects cannot get out. When they struggle, they agitate the water. This alerts the water striders to catch and devour them. You can see this for yourself by sitting motionless for a few minutes at the side of a shallow pond on a warm day. Use a stick to create tiny vibrations (or capture a housefly and throw it in) to attract a water strider's attention.

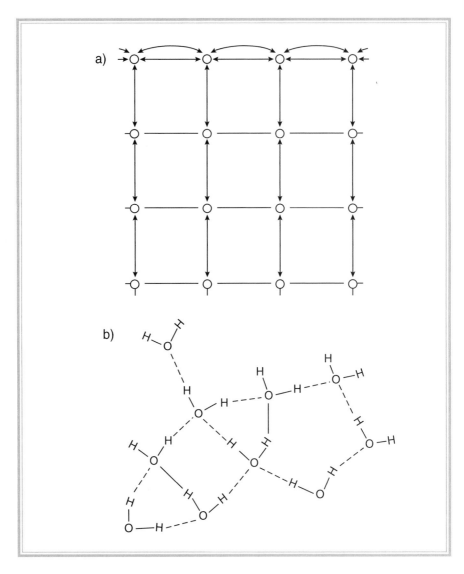

Figure 9. Attractions between molecules of a liquid lead to surface tension. a) In a liquid, the molecules are equally attracted to the other molecules around them except at the surface. At the surface, the attractions between molecules become stronger because there are no liquid molecules above to balance the forces. This causes surface tension. The attractive networks formed by the liquid molecules may take a variety of shapes. b) The high surface tension of water is due to its composition. The diagram shows how hydrogen atoms in each molecule are bonded strongly to their own oxygen atom but are also attracted to oxygen atoms in nearby water molecules.

Project Ideas and Further Investigations

- Can you make a raft of needles or paper clips floating side by side? What precautions need to be taken? What happens when one paper clip touches another one or touches the wall of the container? How big can you make the raft? Can the entire surface of water in a small container be covered by paper clips butted together? What limits its size? What causes a raft to sink? Explain each of these effects in terms of surface tension.

- Try to float each of the following on water: a small straight pin, a straight pin with a large head, a large straight pin, small and large safety pins, small and large paper clips. What other objects can you cause to float in water? Based on your observations, what characteristics make an object more likely to float? Explain in terms of surface tension.

- How does the shape of a small floating object affect the appearance of the water supporting it? Try different shapes. Draw diagrams of this.

Experiment 3.2

Observing Surface Tension

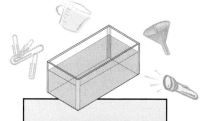

Materials

* empty food can, open at the top
* an adult
* hammer
* large nail
* fish tank or any large container with or without water
* cup of water
* scissors
* sheet of paper

Obtain an empty metal can open at the top. **With the supervision of an adult**, hammer in a large nail to make a hole in the side of the can about an inch above the bottom.

Make two more holes near the first in a horizontal row. The holes should be evenly spaced (see Figure 10a).

Hold the can above a fish tank and fill it with water. You will see separate streams coming out of the holes.

Combine the streams into one by directing the jets of water together with your thumb and forefinger. How can you break the combined stream into single ones again?

When you pinch the jets of water, surface tension holds the combined streams together. If you brush them apart with your hand, the individual surface tensions will take over and keep the streams separate. Similarly, wetting the hairs of an artist's paintbrush allows the bristles to be smoothed to a fine point. Flicking the point with a finger splays out the bristles.

Try the following for another demonstration of surface tension.

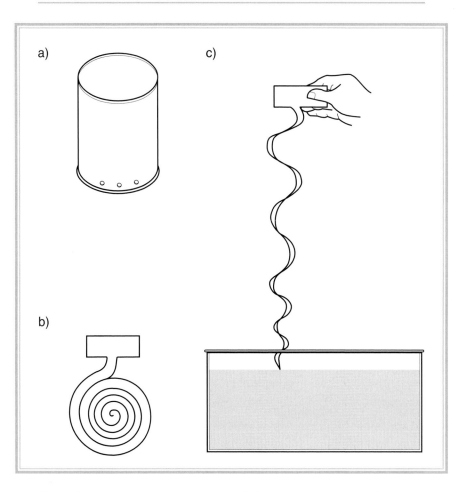

Figure 10. OBSERVING SURFACE TENSION. a) A can, open at the top, has three holes at the bottom. b) Diagram of paper spiral to be cut. c) Lower the end of the spiral to touch the surface of the water.

Cut a paper spiral with a little handle on it, as shown in Figure 10b. The handle can be about two inches wide and the spiral may have as many turns in it as you can make conveniently.

Hold the paper by the handle and make the other end touch the water surface. See Figure 10c. Then, pull the spiral upward.

You will find that you have to jerk the paper upward to get it free of the water. The spiral acts like a paper spring once it touches the water and can only be pulled free with a bounce back up. You can feel the strength of the surface tension.

Project Idea and Further Investigation

When a stream of water falls onto the center of a disk supported by a thin rod, the water will spread out from the center to fall off as a transparent sheet. It is possible to set this up so that the sheet closes back under the disk to form a bell shape. Explain this occurrence in terms of surface tension. Investigate how to change the shape of the descending sheet.

Experiment 3.3

Measuring Surface Tension

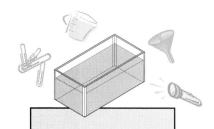

There are a number of different scientific procedures used to measure surface tension. Some measure the force needed to submerge a solid length floating on a liquid. This experiment is a simple variation of this method and can be used to compare surface tensions of different liquids.

Cut a 2-in square of thin, rigid plastic such as vinyl. Float it on the surface of the water in the fish tank. Pile small weights on the plastic to find out how much weight the surface can bear until the plastic sinks. If you do not have commercial weights, you can use convenient multiples of one of the following:

- Straight pin. . . . . 0.0026 oz

- Newspaper, 10 square pieces cut 1 in to a side . . . . 0.012 oz

- No. 1 paper clip . . . . 0.061 oz

- Dime, new . . . . 0.088 oz

- Nickel, new. . . . . 0.18 oz

In an experiment using a 2-in square of high-density polyethylene plastic (#2 in the environmental waste disposal system) it was found that 10 No. 1 paper clips weighing a total of 0.61 oz were needed to sink the square in water.

Once the weight needed to sink the plastic square in water is known, you can compare it to the weight needed to sink the same plastic square in other liquids. The greater the weight needed, the greater the surface tension of the liquid.

Project Ideas and Further Investigations

Do not use a fish tank with fish in it to do any experiments that use any liquid other than water. Do not use a fish tank with fish in it to do experiments using water with solids added.

- Does surface tension increase as the size of the plastic square in Experiment 3.3 is increased? Use successively longer strips until the biggest strip is almost as long as the fish tank. Are there any differences indicated between the surface tensions? If there are differences, do they increase or decrease as the length becomes greater? Suggest explanations.

- Compare the surface tension of water to that of other liquids using the same plastic square as in Experiment 3.3. Compare the results. Which liquid has the strongest attractions between molecules? Which has the weakest attractions? Make up a table that lists the liquids in order of the force of their surface tensions.

- How does surface tension change with temperature? If you use a fish tank with live fish in it for this purpose, you should lower the temperature of the water rather than raise it. Also, check with your local pet store to find the safe range of temperature for your fish.

- How does the surface tension of pure water compare to that of water when it has substances dissolved in it such as sugar or salt? (Do not try this in a tank containing fish.) Invent a hypothesis to explain the results.

- A rubber band floats when placed gently on water but sinks after it is pushed under the water. Formulate a hypothesis to explain this and devise experiments to test your hypothesis.

- Another household method for measuring surface tension uses a double-pan balance. A stick balanced on a pivot can be used for the balance beam. Suspend a square of rigid plastic horizontally by string from each end of the stick. Balance the stick by moving one of the squares as needed. To take measurements, lower one side to the water until the vinyl is wet on the bottom. Place weights on the other side until the square just pulls free. Compare the results obtained this way with the results obtained in Experiment 3.3. Explain any difference.

Experiment 3.4

Will the Water Spill Out?

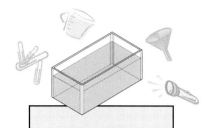

Fill two glasses with water and place one upside down over the other, rim to rim, so that no water spills out. You can do this easily if you do it underwater in the fish tank.

Set the two joined glasses down in a sink so that the bottom one is upright. Slide a coin between the rims. Does the water spill out? You can substitute a toothpick for the coin if you are nervous about doing it without spilling.

Fill a glass of water just to the top. Add drops of water gently to the filled glass until the water spills over. What do you observe? How is this explained by surface tension?

Obtain a small plastic grid basket like the ones used for berries from the fruit counter of your supermarket. Do you think that the water will come through the holes when you place it on the surface of water in the fish tank? Try it. What happens?

Add one drop of liquid soap or detergent to the water next to the basket. (Never add soap or detergent to an operating fish tank.) If nothing happens, stir the water a bit. What happens now?

When the glasses are stacked rim to rim with water inside, surface tension keeps the water from spilling out if a narrow opening is made between the rims. This is what happened when the coin was inserted to keep the rims slightly apart.

When additional water is added one drop at a time to a glass filled with water just to the rim, the additional drops merge with the water. As each additional drop is added, the surface gradually rises up to form a dome. Eventually the surface tension is not enough to contain the rising dome and the water spills over. Soap or detergent in clean water lowers surface tension. When either is added to water, the plastic basket will sink.

Project Idea and Further Investigation

What happens when a drop of detergent is placed in clean water next to a floating pin? In a glass that has been filled with water until it has a dome on the top? Directly behind a flattened strip of aluminum foil several inches long floating on water? Onto water that has had pepper sprinkled on it? Look up the chemical theory that explains how soap lowers surface tension. How does soap act to clean dirty clothes? Why shouldn't it be added to an operating fish tank?

Chapter 4

Cohesion, Adhesion, and Capillary Action

A liquid may take a huge variety of shapes. It may, for example, spread into a sheet, move in waves, swirl, flow smoothly, toss with turbulence, or scatter in drops. Cohesion is the property that keeps the molecules of a liquid together and, in combination with surface tension, helps to make these many shapes possible. As discussed in Chapter 3, cohesion is the attraction that exists between molecules in a liquid.

Adhesion is the attraction between a liquid and any solid that it touches. It is the property that causes a raindrop to stick to a windowpane and bubbles of air to adhere to the side of the bathtub. It helps liquids to stay in containers, and it is necessary for capillary action to take place. Capillary action may sound to you as if it is about the circulation of blood in the body and,

indeed, it helps the pumping action of the heart. However, capillary action is more than that.

Capillary action moves water through narrow spaces. It moves water with dissolved nutrients through the soil so that plants can grow. It helps carry tree sap to where it is needed in a tree, even up to its very top. It is capillary action that helps a paper towel wipe up a spill and helps materials to become wet. Capillary action depends on cohesion, adhesion, and surface tension—all three of them. In this chapter, experiments will demonstrate the causes and effects of cohesion, adhesion, and capillary action.

Experiment 4.1

Cohesion Versus Adhesion

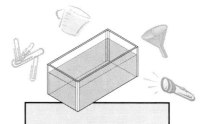

Cohesion and adhesion can be observed in any liquid where it contacts a solid surface.

At eye level, look at the surface of the water where it meets the corner of the fish tank. Is the water surface flat? How does it appear?

Place a wax candle halfway into the water. What does the surface of the water look like where it meets the candle?

Materials

* fish tank or any large rectangular transparent glass container filled with water

* smooth wax candle, at least ½-in diameter

* 2 flat glass plates (no sharp edges) or microscope slides

As shown in Figure 11, the water surface curves upward where it meets the glass. Where its surface contacts the candle, the water curves downward. What is the cause of this difference?

Whether a liquid surface curves up or down on contact with a solid depends upon which is stronger, cohesion within the liquid or adhesion between the liquid and solid. If adhesion is stronger, it pulls the liquid surface upward until the adhesion-cohesion forces are balanced. This is what happens when water meets glass. Glass is made up largely of a network of silicon and oxygen atoms. The oxygen atoms in glass attract the hydrogen atoms of the water, resulting in a fairly strong adhesive force that is stronger than the cohesive force of water.

The adhesive force between water and wax, however, is not as strong as the cohesive forces within water. As a result, the

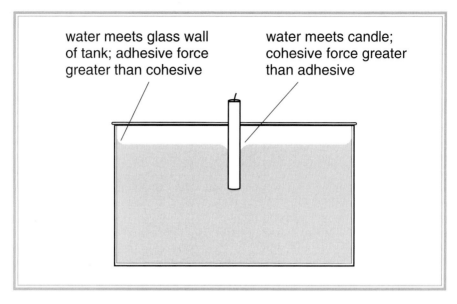

water meets glass wall
of tank; adhesive force
greater than cohesive

water meets candle;
cohesive force greater
than adhesive

Figure 11. COHESIVE FORCE VERSUS ADHESIVE FORCE. Water meets glass wall of tank; adhesive force is greater than cohesive force. Water meets candle; cohesive force is greater than adhesive force.

water pulls away from the wax. It curves downward where they meet. A wax candle is made up mostly of carbon atoms strongly linked to hydrogen atoms or other carbon atoms. The wax has little, if any, attraction to water.

Wet two clean flat glass plates or slides. Place one directly on the other. Now try to pull them apart. How can you separate the pieces of glass?

When you try to pull the glass plates apart, the adhesive forces between water and both glass surfaces resist you. You have to slide one of the plates away from the other until the surfaces in contact are small enough to allow you to pry them apart.

Experiment 4.2

Pouring Water Down a String

Can water be poured down a string set at a slant without spilling off?

Fill a small pitcher with water. Tie a piece of wet string about 15 inches (40 cm) long to the handle. Then pass the string over the top of the pitcher and across the middle of its lip.

Set the pitcher down close to the fish tank. Pick up the free end of the string. Hold it against the inside of an upper metal frame of the fish tank. Attach it

Materials

* small pitcher
* string about 15 in (40 cm) long
* fish tank or any container with a metal frame
* small magnet

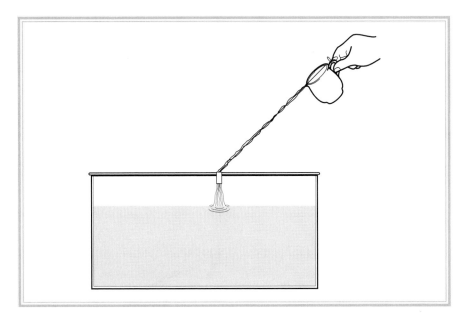

Figure 12. POURING WATER DOWN A STRING

63

with a magnet. Move the pitcher up and hold it so that the string extends at a slant down to the tank without sagging (see Figure 12).

Pour the water slowly out. What happens?

Instead of dropping straight down, the stream of water flows along the string into the fish tank. Adhesive forces bind the descending water to the string. Cohesive forces hold the water together as it moves along the string so that drops of it do not fall away. How can you break the stream of water loose from the string?

Project Ideas and Further Investigations

- Fish tanks often have particles of floating dirt that contaminate the water and need to be removed. A stick can be used to touch the particle and remove it from the water. Investigate what a dipstick is, what it is made of, and what shape is best for it. Explain how it works.

- Based on the curve at the solid-water interface, visually compare solids to find out how strong the adhesive force is. Try materials such as glass, steel, porcelain (as in a mug), polystyrene, Teflon, paraffin, Plexiglas, etc. List the materials in approximate order of their adhesive strength at the water-solid interface.

- The angle that a liquid forms at the interface with its container is called the contact angle. You can roughly measure the contact angle by using a protractor; a magnifying glass helps. What is the size of the contact angle for the water-glass interface? Compare the adhesive strength exerted on water by other solids besides glass by measuring the contact angles. List them in order of their adhesive strength for water. Consider researching the composition of the other solids to explain the differences.

- Compare the adhesive force at the glass-liquid interface for different liquids such as water, alcohol, glycerol, and cooking oil based on the contact angle. List them in order of the adhesive force. Does the contact angle give you information about their cohesive forces?

- Does the adhesive force at the glass/water interface change with temperature?

Experiment 4.3

Causing Water to Flow Upward

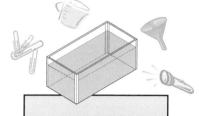

Materials

* * any large container with water
* * bucket or large jar
* * transparent plastic flexible tubing at least 2 ft (60 cm) long
* * optional: giant dropper (baster)
* * optional: clamp

Use a large container without fish in it for this experiment.

Place a large jar or bucket next to and below the water-filled container. Obtain a piece of flexible tubing at least 2 feet (60 cm) long. Fill it completely with water. The tubing should have no air bubbles in it.

There are several ways to completely fill the tubing. Here are two of them.

1. The easiest way is to use a clean giant dropper. It is sold as a baster in the kitchen section of grocery, hardware, or dollar stores. Place one end of the tubing into the water-filled container with the other end hanging out. Squeeze the bulb of the dropper to empty it of air and place the tip into the water in the tank. Release the bulb so that the dropper fills with water. Push the tip of the dropper into the end of the tubing that is outside the tank. Squeeze the bulb to fill the tube completely with water and let it drive out all the air. Pinch the tubing to close it tightly below the dropper or close it with a clamp. Disconnect the dropper from the tubing. There should be no air bubbles in the tubing. Go on to the next step.

2. Attach one end of the tubing to a faucet and place the other end at the bottom of the partly-filled container. Run a

stream of water into the tubing until no more air comes out. Pinch tightly or clamp the faucet end of the tubing. Leave the other end under water in the container. Disconnect the tubing from the faucet. Go on to the next step.

At this point, one end of the tubing is open at the bottom of the tank and the other is outside the tank and clamped closed. Pull the closed end so that the tubing extends over the

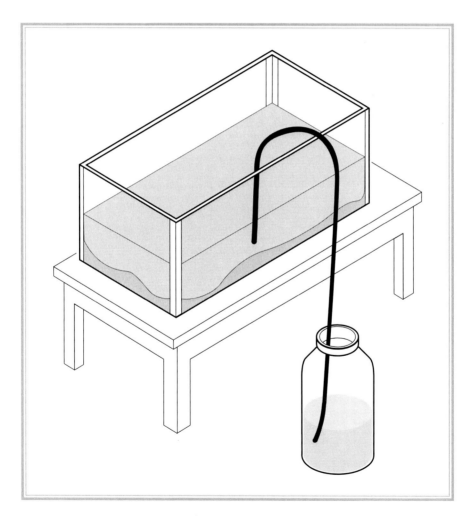

Figure 13. AN OPERATING SIPHON

top of the tank and down into the jar below. Open the end in the jar.

Water will flow from the tank up the tube and down the other side. If it doesn't, you probably have an air bubble in the tubing. Refill it and repeat the process. Once the water is flowing, you have made a siphon (see Figure 13). Why does a siphon work?

The explanation involves a combination of causes. Although it is often believed that the water is pushed over the top by air pressure, this is disproved by the simple fact that a siphon works in a vacuum. A siphon works after you have provided the initial energy needed to get the water up the tubing and over the top of the tank. The weight of water in the tubing going into the jar is greater than that of the water in the shorter part of the tubing that goes to the tank. It is this imbalance of weight that powers the continuing flow of the siphon. Cohesive forces keep the water from breaking apart as it flows over the arch. Adhesive forces help by pulling the water to the sides. The siphon will work as long as the water level in the catch bucket is below the water level in the tank. Once the catch bucket is nearly full, lift it up until the siphon stops to prevent a mess.

Experiment 4.4

Experimenting with a Siphon

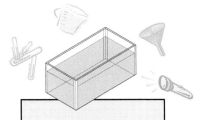

Materials

* fish tank without fish in it or other large container with water

* bucket or large jar

* transparent plastic flexible tubing at least 1 ft (30 cm) long and another piece at least about 5 ft (150 cm) long

* optional: giant dropper (baster)

Completely fill with water a length of tubing about 5 feet (150 cm) as described in Experiment 4.3 and start a siphon operating from a filled fish tank into a bucket or jar.

Lift up the bucket or jar into which the siphon is emptying until it is above the water level in the fish tank. Be sure that the ends of the tubing remain underwater throughout. What do you observe? After a short time, lower the jar until it is below the fish tank. Which way does the water move now? Try siphoning back and forth.

Raise the jar until the water level in the jar is slightly above the water level in the fish tank. How long does the siphon continue to operate?

Raise the jar again until it is completely above the fish tank. How long does the siphon continue to operate? When it stops, what do you observe has happened to the column of water on each side of the siphon?

Restart your siphon. Does the siphon work if the tubing droops below the catch bucket before entering it? Does the siphon work if the tubing has some loops in it above the tank? Can you make the siphon work with the 5-foot length of tubing looped as high up as possible?

What happens to the siphon if the end in the fish tank flips above the water?

When the jar is momentarily lifted above the fish tank, the siphon reverses direction, going from the jar to the fish tank. When the jar is placed below the fish tank, the siphon again reverses direction, this time withdrawing water from the fish tank. Then, when the water level in the jar is set higher than that in the fish tank, the siphon continues until both water levels are equal. At that point it stops, but it can be restarted if the jar is raised or lowered.

When the jar is raised above the fish tank and allowed to continue operating, its action continues until the jar is empty. At that point the water column breaks and the siphon stops.

An operating siphon continues to work no matter how many loops are made in the tubing. The siphon works with a higher arch, too. If the end of the tubing in the fish tank flips out of the water, the column of water is broken and the siphon stops operating.

If you were to allow the siphon to continue operating, it would empty the fish tank. This is probably the safest way to empty a fish tank. Of course, you would need to empty it into a larger container than the jar.

Project Ideas and Further Investigations

*In all experiments that require working from a window, ladder, or stairwell, be sure to have **adult supervision**.*

- Construct a siphon so that it runs from the fish tank to the ceiling and back again. Does it continue to operate? Run a siphon hose around the room before feeding it into the receiving container. Does it still continue to operate? Why?

- Does the speed of flow of a siphon depend upon the diameter of the tubing? Make a hypothesis and conduct experiments to test it.

- Design experiments to determine whether the speed of flow of a siphon depends upon the maximum height that the siphon tubing reaches above the water surface in the tank.

- Make a hypothesis and design experiments to find whether differences in height between the water levels in the upper and receiving containers in a siphon affect the speed of flow. Graph the rate of flow versus the difference in height and interpret the results.

- Design an experiment to check whether any outside air pressure is needed to operate a siphon. To explain the results, it may be helpful to look in physics books and physics magazines for information on the topic.

- A modern toilet uses a siphon mechanism. Make a diagram showing how it works. What determines the height of the siphon? Suggest modifications and the possible consequences.

Experiment 4.5

Capillary Action

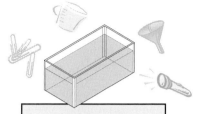

Materials

＊ fish tank or any large rectangular transparent glass container filled with water

＊ glass tube with about a ¼-in opening

＊ glass tube with opening wider than ¼ in

Vertically lower a glass tube with a ¼-inch opening until it is partway into the water in a fish tank. Look at the water surface inside the tube. Is it flat? How does its level compare with that of the water outside the tube?

Repeat the observation but use glass tubing with a wider opening. Compare the results.

When glass tubing is lowered into water, the water rises up in it until it is higher than the level of the water surface outside the tube. Not only is the column of water higher, but the water is even higher at the edges all around. The increase in height is not as great when the tube is wider. The term used to describe this occurrence is *capillary action.*

Capillary action is not a simple phenomenon. Essentially, it is due to a combination of adhesion, surface tension, and cohesion. In a glass tube, adhesive forces act from all sides on the narrow column of water. The adhesive forces pull the water upward along the glass. Cohesion pulls the molecules of water together so that the water rises as a column without a break. Surface tension keeps the surface from breaking. Gravity pulls the water downward. The water rises until the upward adhesive pull is balanced by the downward force of gravity on the water: the water's weight.

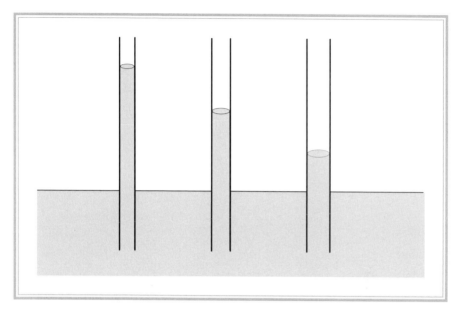

Figure 14. CAPILLARY ACTION IN NARROW TUBES OF DIFFERENT DIAMETERS

The narrower the glass tube, the higher up the water goes (see Figure 14). This is because the adhesive force in a narrow tube increases at a faster rate than the weight of the water does.

Experiment 4.6

Capillary Action Between Two Glass Plates

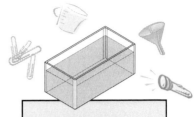

Hinge two glass plates or microscope slides together with a piece of transparent tape. Large plates of flat glass show the capillary effect better than small ones. Hold the glass plates vertically and place them partway into the water in the fish tank as shown in Figure 15.

Materials

* fish tank or any large rectangular transparent glass container filled with water

* 2 glass plates flat on each side (no sharp edges) or microscope slides

* transparent tape

* toothpick

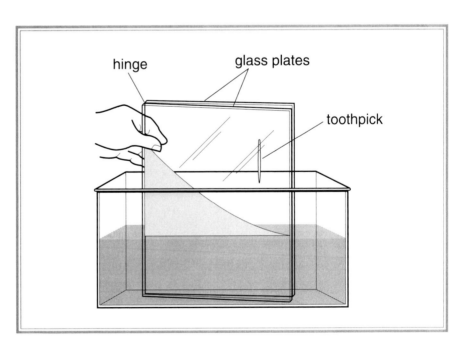

Figure 15. Water rises between two glass plates due to capillary action.

On the side opposite the hinge, slip the point of a toothpick between the plates. While slipping the toothpick in a little further, gradually tilt it upward until it is vertical.

You will observe the water rising upward in a curve away from the toothpick side. The closer the glass plates, the higher the water rises. The toothpick lessens the effect of the capillary action by increasing the distance between the plates.

Project Ideas and Further Investigations

- Use the method in Experiment 4.6 to investigate what determines the strength of the capillary action of the liquid between the glass plates. You may wish to improve the experiment to make it more precise. Try different liquids such as vegetable oil or rubbing alcohol. (You might want to use smaller containers for these liquids.) Consider the properties of the liquid such as density, viscosity, and composition to see what makes the difference, if any.
- Does a solute dissolved in water affect the strength of the capillary action between glass plates? Try different solutes such as sugar and salt, then try different concentrations of the solute.
- Explain how capillary action in narrow blood vessels improves the pumping action of the heart. Consult books and articles to help find the answer.

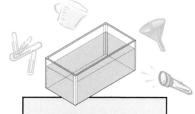

Experiment 4.7

Using a Towel to Move Water

Cut a strip of cloth toweling about 1 inch (3 cm) wide and 12 inches (30 cm) long. Twist the strip all along its length to make a continuous spiral. You can instead use a paper towel rolled into a narrow tube and then flattened.

Place a drinking glass next to the fish tank so that the top of the glass is a little higher than the water level in the fish tank (see Figure 16). If necessary, prop the glass up on a box or other support.

Materials

* fish tank or any large container filled with water to an inch below the top

* strip of cotton cloth toweling about 1–2 in (3–4 cm) wide and about 12 in (30 cm) long, or sheet of paper towel

* drinking glass

* optional: box or other support

Bend the toweling over the rim of a drinking glass so that no more than 1 inch (2–3 cm) hangs into the glass. Lead the other end of the strip into the water in the fish tank. The strip should not sag between the rim of the glass and the rim of the tank. It does not matter how much of the strip ends up submerged in the water in the fish tank. Examine the glass every hour or so. What happens in the empty glass?

How much water can be transferred to the glass?

You will find that the strip becomes completely wet. The water climbs up from the fish tank and over along the toweling. Soon, water drips off the end of the toweling down into the glass below it. The water continues to drip until the water levels in the glass and the tank are equal.

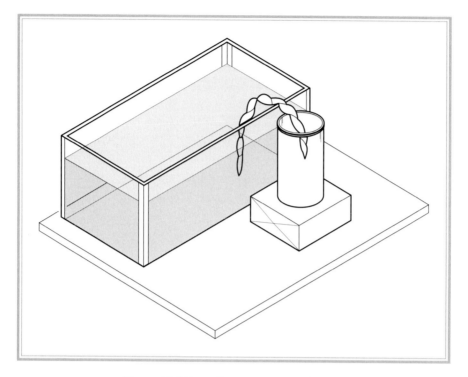

Figure 16. Water flows up a twisted cloth.

The adhesive force between the water and the towel is large enough to pull the water up the towel in spite of gravity. The pores and narrow spaces in the cloth increase adhesion by increasing the surface to which the water can adhere. This is capillary action.

Project Ideas and Further Investigations

- Compare the capillary action of water in glass tubing to that of water in tubes of other transparent materials. Pet fish stores and hardware stores carry tubing of different types of plastic. Transparent plastic straws can also be tested.

- Graph the relationship between the diameter of a tube (glass or plastic) and the height that water rises in the tube when it is placed partway into water. Describe the relationship based on your graph.
- Investigate how width, thickness, or number of folds in a cloth or paper strip affects the volume of water that moves during a specified length of time from the fish tank to a glass next to it.
- Construct a hypothesis on how to empty a glass of water into an empty glass by using a paper towel and then test it by an experiment.
- Can the use of a towel to move water be applied to filter dirty water? Try it. If it works, suggest how this method can be applied to solve dirty water problems in the home or in a factory.
- When someone walks on wet sand, the footprints appear dry. This effect is called dilatancy. An explanation given for this is based, in part, on surface tension and capillarity. Investigate this phenomenon.
- Paper chromatography is a very useful method for separating chemicals or analyzing for the presence of certain chemicals. It depends on competition between cohesion and adhesion. The process is described in many chemistry books. Use the library to find out how to carry out some of these experiments in the home. Add your own variations. Explain how paper chromatography works using the adhesion-cohesion theory.

Chapter 5

Pressure in a Fish Tank

Air and water pressure are very important to life on this planet. In our oceans, for example, are myriads of underwater creatures. Each type of creature can exist comfortably only within a narrow range of depths. This is because water pressure changes with depth. Pressure within the ocean increases the lower one descends from the surface. The differences in water pressure keep the occupants of one layer from mixing with those in other layers.

Above the oceans, the earth is surrounded by a blanket of air that thins out with height. Gravity holds this air to the earth. Like water pressure in the oceans, air pressure increases the closer one gets to the surface of the earth. Passengers in airplanes can feel the increase in air pressure in their ears as a plane descends. The fact that air has weight was not discovered until many centuries after civilization first flourished. Even now, when we know that air presses down on us with a force of 14.7 pounds on every square inch, it is hard to believe that it is so strong. That is because we do not feel the air pressing down on us. We do not cave in under air pressure for a very good reason: the air and fluids in our bodies exert an equal pressure back.

Air pressure is exerted upon every exposed substance within our atmosphere, including liquids—upon the oceans as well as upon the water in a fish tank. When swimming in a pool, we are unaware of either air pressure on the water or pressure from the water around us. Yet we know that humans who descend into the ocean must be aware of the dangers due to increases in pressure with depth. A submarine that is not built to withstand tremendous water pressure will be destroyed at low ocean depths. Deep-sea divers must have a breathing apparatus that allows their lungs to expand to inhale air. They also must be very careful to ascend slowly to give their blood systems time to adjust to the pressure changes.

The experiments in this chapter will examine some of the properties of air and water pressure.

Experiment 5.1

Water Exerts Pressure

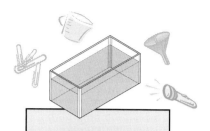

Materials

* fish tank, any large container, or a sink
* 1-liter (or larger) plastic soft drink bottle
* an adult
* water
* long nail
* hammer
* masking tape
* chunk of clay about the size of your thumb
* hard smooth surface
* pencil with eraser on it
* heavy book

Obtain an empty 1-liter (or larger) plastic soft drink bottle. **With adult supervision**, use a nail and hammer to punch four holes into the bottle in a *vertical* row about the same distance apart from each other. Seal the holes with one long strip of masking tape. Fill the bottle with water.

Hold the bottle firmly by its neck above the fish tank as you pull off the tape. Observe the water as it exits from the four holes. What evidence do you see that water is exerting pressure? How can you tell where the water pressure is strongest? Where is it weakest?

You will find that the water leaps out of the bottom hole almost horizontally (see Figure 17). The stream of water coming out of the next higher hole slopes downward a little. The stream droops coming out of the hole above that, and just falls out of the highest hole.

Since all else is the same, the differences in the way the water falls can only be due to the weight of the water above the holes. The weight exerts a downward force. The more water above a spot, the greater the force it exerts on the spot.

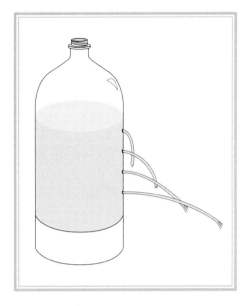

Figure 17. Water exerts pressure, which increases with depth.

The greater the force, the greater the pressure of the water at that spot.

Scientifically, *pressure* is defined as force divided by the area on which it acts. This means that pressure depends both on force and on the area over which the force is spread. The following experiment illustrates the difference between force and pressure.

Press a small chunk of clay down on a hard smooth surface and flatten it. Place a pencil point down on top of the clay. With one hand, gently keep the pencil vertical but do not push the pencil into the clay. With the other hand, place a heavy book on the pencil. Allow the pencil to sink into the clay under the weight of the book. Remove the book and pencil. Place the pencil with its point upward on top of another flat spot on the clay. Again, keep the pencil standing vertically, this time on its eraser. Place the heavy book on top of the point and allow the pencil to sink into the clay under the weight of the book. Remove the book and pencil.

Which was pushed deeper into the clay, the point or the eraser?

The force (weight of the book) acting upon the pencil is the same in both cases. Why does the pointed end sink in deeper than the eraser? The area of the rounded eraser end is much larger than the area of the sharp pencil tip. As a result, the force on the eraser end is spread over a greater area. Since the force on the pencil point acts on a smaller area, the pressure there is greater and the pencil point is pushed in deeper.

Project Ideas and Further Investigations

- Does water pressure depend upon the shape of the container? Does it depend upon the diameter of the container? Investigate these questions. Consider using different sizes and shapes of plastic bottles as in Experiment 5.1 or of cans as in Experiment 3.2 to help find the answers.
- Is the water pressure the same at different spots in a container as long as they are at the same level? Again, consider using an empty plastic bottle or can to help find the answer.
- Suppose you have a tall container with a hole in its side very close to the bottom. If you lift the container over a sink and fill it with water, a stream will pour out and hit the bottom of the sink. As the container empties, what happens to the horizontal distance at which the stream lands? Devise an explanation. Consider also taking measurements of water height in the container and horizontal impact distance to make a graph that can provide additional information.

Experiment 5.2

Upward Water Pressure

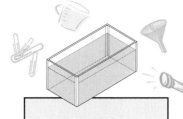

Obtain a juice can open at both ends. From a plastic lid such as those used for margarine tubs, cut a square large enough to cover one end of the can. Sink the can, covered end down, partway into the water in a fish tank. Let go of the plastic square. Does the square stay in place? Why?

Holding the can in the same position, slowly pour water into the can until the square floats loose. When does that happen? Why?

When the can is placed into the water and held there, the plastic square stays in place. The water beneath the plastic must be pushing it upward. Evidently, water can exert an upward pressure.

If the downward pressure were to be increased until it equaled the upward pressure on the plastic square, the square should float loose. You gradually increased the downward pressure by adding water to the can. The square floated loose when the water levels inside and outside the can became equal.

This result will be investigated further by using a manometer. The next experiment will show you how to make a manometer.

Experiment 5.3

Measuring Pressure

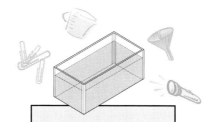

Materials

* 2 lengths of flexible rubber or plastic tubing that fit the straws tightly, one about 6 in (15 cm) long and the other at least 2 ft (60 cm) long

* 2 transparent glass or plastic drinking straws

* masking tape

* block of wood at least 14 in (36 cm) long

* water

* food coloring

* small plastic, metal, or glass funnel

* scissors

* piece of thin rubber sheet (cut from a balloon) large enough to fit over the mouth of the funnel

* optional: rubber band

A manometer is a device for measuring pressure. You can make one like the one shown in Figure 18.

Use tubing that is about 6 inches (15 cm) in length to connect two transparent glass or plastic straws. Fit one end of a 2-foot- (60-cm-) long piece of tubing tightly on to the free end of one of the straws. Use masking tape to mount the straw assembly in a large U-shape on the block of wood.

Make some colored water. Insert the small end of a funnel into the free end of the long tubing. Pour colored water into the funnel until the straws are filled about halfway. Disconnect the funnel from the tubing.

Cut a circle out of a thin rubber sheet large enough to cover the mouth of the funnel. Stretch the rubber circle tightly over the entire mouth of the funnel and hold it in place with a rubber band or masking tape.

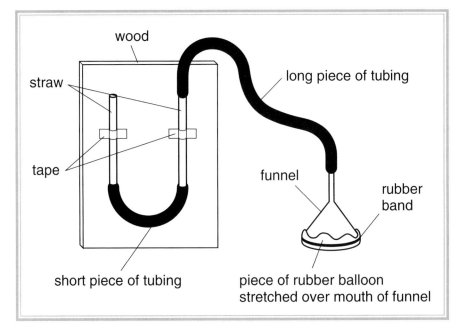

Figure 18. A manometer measures pressure.

Fit the free end of the long piece of tubing tightly over the small end of the funnel.

You have made a manometer. The manometer can be used to compare water pressure at various spots within a filled fish tank.

Pick up the funnel end of the manometer and gently press on the rubber sheet with the palm of your hand. What change do you see in the manometer? Remove your hand. What change do you observe now? Explain.

When you pressed on the rubber sheet, you pushed on the air inside the funnel. This push moved air through the rubber tubing and onto the water in the straw. The air pushed the water down, which pushed the water up an equal amount on the other side. When you removed your hand, everything went back to where it was.

You can tell just from looking at the difference in water levels when there is an increase in pressure. If you were to blow into the open end of the U-tube, what do you think would happen?

You were correct if you said that the water would rise on the funnel side.

Experiment 5.4

How Does Water Pressure Change with Depth?

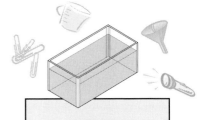

Materials

✳ fish tank or any large rectangular transparent container filled with water

✳ manometer made in Experiment 5.3

Use the manometer you made in Experiment 5.3 to observe changes in water pressure when you place the mouth of the funnel downward at different depths in the fish tank (see Figure 19a).

Keeping the funnel mouth downward at the same level all the time, move the funnel back and forth just below the surface. Does the water pressure change? Move the funnel, still holding the funnel mouth down, from side to side. Does the pressure change now?

Pick a spot about halfway between the surface of the water and the bottom of the tank. Keep the center of the funnel mouth at the same spot while you turn the funnel mouth up, down, to one side, and then to the other side (see Figure 19b). Does the water pressure change during these changes? Repeat this at a different depth.

As the funnel descends into the water, the water level goes down in the side of the U-tube attached to the funnel and up on the other side. This means that the pressure has increased, and confirms what was observed in Experiment 5.1: Water pressure increases with depth. This makes sense, since the greater the height of water above a spot, the greater the weight of water on that spot.

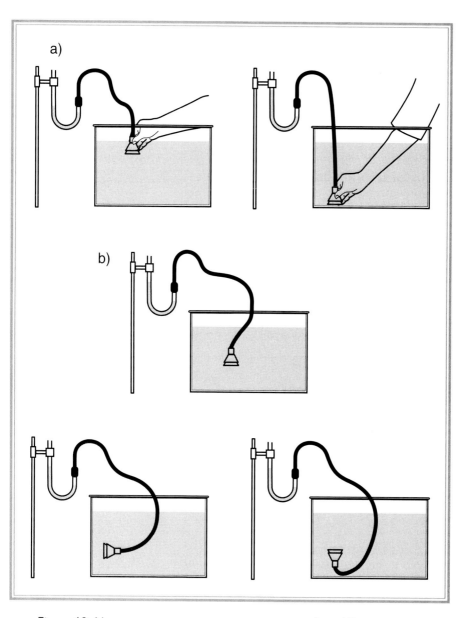

Figure 19. Use a manometer to measure pressures a) at different depths and b) at the same depth from different directions.

When the funnel is moved to different places at the same depth, the pressure remains the same as long as the depth remains the same. Water pressure is the same at the same depth.

Whether the funnel is directly below or directly above the same spot, the manometer shows that the pressure is the same. When the funnel is rotated in place, the water levels in the manometer stay the same. The pressure on a point in a liquid is the same from all directions.

Experiment 5.5

Pascal's Law

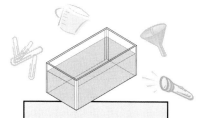

Pascal's law (Blaise Pascal, 1623–1662) says that when pressure is applied to an enclosed fluid, the pressure is transmitted equally throughout the entire fluid. The fluid can be a liquid or a gas. To help understand what this means, try the following.

Materials
✳ balloon or plastic bag (one or two, as needed)
✳ tie to seal balloon or bag
✳ fish tank or any large container filled with water
✳ towel
✳ large pin

Fill a balloon or plastic bag with water and tie it tightly closed. Lower it under the surface of the water in a fish tank. While the balloon is in the water, apply pressure with your fingers to any one spot. Does the balloon bulge out elsewhere? Does this agree with Pascal's law?

Remove the balloon and dry it. Hold it over the tank while quickly puncturing holes with a pin around its middle. If water does not come out of the pinholes, surface tension may be sealing the holes. In that case, squeeze on the neck of the balloon to get jets of water coming out. Next, squeeze harder on the neck of the balloon. Do the jets increase equally all around or do you see differences? Are your observations in agreement with Pascal's law?

When the water-filled balloon is submerged, pressure on it at one spot causes the balloon to bulge a little all around. That is, the pressure due to a push on one spot spreads evenly throughout the water in the balloon. This is as predicted by Pascal's law.

When the water-filled balloon is pricked with pinholes around its middle, water jets spurt evenly out of the holes around the balloon (unless the pinholes are so small that surface tension seals the holes). When pressure is increased at the neck, the jets of water that come out all spurt evenly farther out. In agreement with Pascal's law, the increase in pressure on squeezing the balloon has been transmitted equally throughout the water.

Project Ideas and Further Investigations

- Attach rulers to the wood support of your manometer so that a ruler sits behind each tube. Thin plastic rulers are best for this. You can use this calibrated manometer to measure the differences in height between the two arms of the U-tube. Consult introductory physics books to find out how to read the pressure from your manometer. Develop a hypothesis to explain what happens to the pressure as the depth in water increases. Conduct an experiment to check your hypothesis. A laundry sink or bathtub will allow you to measure to depths of several feet. Perhaps you can obtain permission to use a swimming pool **under adult supervision**. Graph the relationship between depth and pressure. What does the graph tell you?

- Use the calibrated manometer to compare changes in pressure with depth for water to that of other liquids such as rubbing alcohol or sugar solutions of different concentrations. Suggest an explanation for any differences you observe.

- Pascal's law is applied to many hydraulic devices used in industry. Search for information on these devices and diagram how they work.

- Make a hydraulic device that applies Pascal's law to lift a heavy weight using a force that is smaller than the downward force exerted by the heavy weight.

Experiment 5.6
Air Pressure: Putting a Glass into Water Without Filling It Up

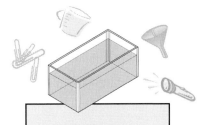

Materials

* fish tank or any large transparent container filled with water
* drinking glass
* towel
* small ball of crumpled aluminum foil
* cardboard

Turn a glass upside down and lower it into the water, mouth down. What do you observe? Slowly tip the glass to one side. What evidence do you see that something was in the glass? What was the something? Remove the glass and dry it.

Float a small ball of crumpled aluminum foil on the water in the tank. Wedge a piece of cardboard into the bottom of the upright glass so that the cardboard stays in place even when the glass is turned over. Turn the glass upside down. Press the mouth of the glass slowly down over the ball of foil until you have pushed the glass to the bottom of the tank. Be sure not to let any of the air in the glass escape. See Figure 20.

What happens to the foil? Does the cardboard get wet? Can you get the foil to touch the cardboard? Is air heavier or lighter than water?

When a glass is lowered mouth down into water, the glass does not fill up. Evidently, something invisible inside the glass is keeping the water back. The invisible something is the air trapped in it. The trapped air presses upon the water and prevents the water from entering the glass. The bubbles

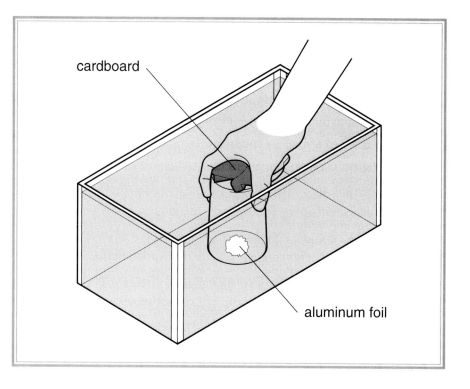

cardboard

aluminum foil

Figure 20. You can put a glass into water without filling it up.

that emerge when the glass is tipped upward are bubbles of air. The escaping air is lighter than water.

When the inverted glass is pushed to the bottom of the tank, the trapped air in it continues to keep the water out. As a result, the foil floating on the surface of the water under the glass remains on the surface all the way down to the bottom. The cardboard inside the top of the glass stays there and remains dry. The foil never gets any closer to the cardboard.

Evidently, air can exert pressure. You have probably put your hand out the window of a moving car and felt the pressure of the air rushing past. Wind on your face is made of air pushing on you.

Air exerts pressure when its molecules bombard a surface. Even though the molecules are very small, there are billions of them in even a tiny space. These molecules move very fast. All of them together can exert quite a bit of pressure when they bang a surface. When you blow into a balloon, for example, the molecules of your breath exert enough force on the skin of the balloon to push it out.

Project Idea and Further Investigation

Dr. Edmond Halley (1656–1742)—the same one for whom the comet is named—invented the earliest modern diving bell in 1690. A diving bell is a structure that is open at the bottom end. It is lowered into deep water with the open end down. It works on the same principle as the drinking glass in Experiment 5.6. Construction operators can work underwater in the enclosed air. Build a small-scale model diving bell and use it to demonstrate how a diving bell operates. What precautions must be taken for the safety of the workers using the bell?

Experiment 5.7

Upward Air Pressure in Water

We have seen that enclosed air exerts pressure on water. However, the pressure of the enclosed air is not the only air pressure that acts upon water in the tank.

Lower a drinking glass into a sink and allow it to fill with water.

Materials

* any large container or a sink filled with water

* transparent drinking glass

* waxed paper

When full, turn it mouth down near the bottom of the tank. Slowly raise the glass until the mouth of the glass is almost up to the surface. Observe.

Will the water still stay in the glass when it is pulled above the water? Try it.

Refill the glass of water. Cover it with a piece of waxed paper. Press down around the paper to seal it tightly to the glass. Over the fish tank or sink, turn the glass carefully upside down while holding the wax paper tightly to the glass. Let go of the paper. What happens?

As the inverted glass is raised up in the water, the water in it also rises without spilling out. When the filled glass is taken all the way out of the water, the water falls right out of it.

Why doesn't the water fall out of the glass as you raise it up in the water almost to the surface? What is holding it up? Believe it or not, it is the air above the tank that is holding up the water in the glass.

The "ocean" of air above us exerts pressure on everything in it. At the beach (sea level), 14.7 pounds of air are pressing on every inch of surface it hits. Pascal's law tells us that any pressure exerted upon water in a tank will be felt equally everywhere within the water. This means that as the atmosphere presses downward upon the water in the tank, that pressure is felt equally and in all directions—including sideways and upwards—through the water in the tank.

What holds the water up in the drinking glass in this experiment is mostly the outside air pressure. The air pressure is transmitted down through the tank and upward to the water in the glass, according to Pascal's law (see Figure 21).

Since atmospheric pressure is pushing upward at 14.7 pounds per square inch, you may be wondering why atmospheric pressure can hold the water in the glass when the

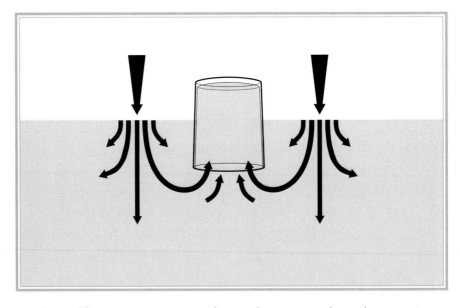

Figure 21. DEMONSTRATING PASCAL'S LAW. Air pressure above the water is shown by the downward arrows. The air pressure pushes downward upon the entire surface of the liquid. The pressure is transmitted with equal force in all directions throughout the liquid.

glass is below the surface but not once the glass is raised into the air.

Although atmospheric pressure exerts sufficient push to hold up the water, it can also push its way right through the water if it gets the chance. It can do this in the same way that your fingers can hold up a lump of chocolate pudding, but you can also push your fingers right into the pudding. When the glass is lifted above the water, the adhesive force between glass and water is enough to cause a bulge in the water surface at the mouth of the glass. As the water surface bulges, air can push into one side of it. When air enters, the water spills out past it.

However, if the water surface is tightly sealed with waxed paper, you can lift the glass into the air without losing the water. The paper prevents the water from bulging unevenly.

Project Ideas and Further Investigations

- In Experiment 5.7, you were able to lift an inverted drinking glass and the water in it almost out of the fish tank water without dropping any of the water. Does the water still stay in if the glass is wider? Find out. Is there a limit as to how wide a container can be used? What is your hypothesis? Explain.
- Supermarkets often sell small cardboard juice containers with a flexible straw that fits tightly into the container. How does your mouth work to get suction on the straw? Is the juice being pulled or pushed through the straw? Can you actually empty the juice container by sucking on the straw without stopping?

Work out each step in the process, diagram it, and add explanations of what is happening.

• Operating fish tanks use an aerator to circulate the water by bubbling air upward. Construct an air pump that works in a fish tank. Consult library books on how a bicycle pump works. You may also find some information there on how to construct an air pump.

• Obtain a water pistol and explain how it works. Change the design to make the jet longer.

Experiment 5.8

How High Can Water Stay Up?

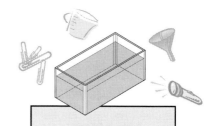

Materials

* ✱ fish tank or any large container filled with water
* ✱ 2-liter plastic bottle
* ✱ transparent flexible rubber or plastic tubing at least 5 ft long
* ✱ optional: giant dropper (baster)
* ✱ an adult
* ✱ optional: chair or ladder
* ✱ measuring tape

Fill a 2-liter plastic bottle with water, cover the mouth of the bottle with your hand, turn it over and lower the bottle into a fish tank. Then remove your hand. Does the water empty out?

The water stays in the bottle. The air pressure pushing upward is greater than the downward pressure of the water.

Suppose the bottle is 5 feet tall. Will the water still stay in it? Suppose it is 50 feet tall. What then? A 50-foot bottle or even a 5-foot one would be hard to find and difficult to handle. However, a length of tubing will work just as well. Transparent flexible plastic or rubber tubing may be purchased from a tropical fish store or from a hardware store.

If there are fish in the tank, it is safer to use a filled bucket as the source for water in this experiment.

Fill a length of tubing with water from end to end. It is important that there be no air bubbles in the tube. See Experiment 4.3 for two ways to get bubble-free water into the tubing.

Cap each end of the tubing firmly with a finger. Lower one end of the tubing to the bottom of a container of water and remove your finger. With your finger still capping the top end, raise the tubing vertically. Be sure that the lower end stays under water throughout. Does the water stay in the tubing? **With the help of an adult**, you may wish to get up on a chair or ladder to raise the tubing higher. How high up are you lifting it?

If you were to take your finger off the top of the tubing, what would happen? Try it.

Theoretically, you can raise the water in the tubing to a maximum height of 34 feet (10.5 m). At that height, the pressure of the water downward equals the upward atmospheric pressure. Above that height, the upward air pressure cannot support any additional weight. If you filled a length of tubing that was 50 feet long and raised it to full height, the water would drop back down to 34 feet high. What would be in the space above the water?

Nothing, literally, would be in the space above the water. A vacuum would exist there.

Project Ideas and Further Investigations

In all projects that require working from a window, ladder, or stairwell, be sure to have **adult supervision.**

- Find the maximum height to which you can raise water in narrow-diameter plastic tubing. If your result differs from the theoretical 34 feet (10.5 m), suggest reasons why. Does the result change if wide-diameter tubing is used instead? Investigate.
- Can a siphon operate at higher than 34 feet? Find articles in the library about this topic. Based on your findings, see if you can get a siphon to work well above 34 feet.
- Several hundred years ago, Otto von Guericke (1602–1686) had a glass tube made that was closed at the top and more than 34 feet high. It was filled with water with the open end down in a large container of water. Guericke had the apparatus set into his house so that it stuck up through the roof and could be seen by the local townspeople. He had made a barometer, an instrument that measures atmospheric pressure. Changes in atmospheric pressure can foretell changes in weather. The townspeople could look at the barometer and forecast the weather. In the library, look up the details of Guericke's barometer. How did it work? What changes in today's barometers have been made so that a more convenient tube length can be used? Find another liquid or solution with a density much greater than that of water that you can safely use to construct a barometer much shorter than the one used by Guericke. Make plans to build such a barometer and bring the plans to your science teacher or other adult.

Chapter 6

Floating and Sinking

The great ship *Titanic* was considered unsinkable. It was the largest ship in the world at the time, weighed 66,000 tons when fully loaded, and was a marvel of engineering. It began its first voyage on April 10, 1912. Four days later at about 11:30 P.M., it struck an iceberg. Over 200 feet of one side was sliced open. At least five supposedly watertight compartments were flooded. The *Titanic* sank at 2:20 A.M. with a loss of about 1,500 lives. Why did it sink? How could a metal ship as huge as the *Titanic* even float when we know that a rock sinks?

The tendency of an object to sink or float in a liquid or air is called buoyancy. It was the great Greek engineer and mathematician Archimedes (around 287–212 B.C.) who first stated the principles of buoyancy. Archimedes was known to concentrate on his work to the point of being described as eccentric and absentminded. It seems that both of these characteristics were in action when he discovered the principle of buoyancy. It is said that he solved the problem during a bath when he saw the tub overflow as he stepped into the water. Delighted to have found the answer, he leaped out of the tub and ran naked through the streets shouting, "Eureka! Eureka!" *Eureka* is the Greek word for "I have found it."

Buoyancy is a topic of major interest in physics. It deals with why ships sink or float, how submarines must be constructed to safely submerge and to rise again, how fish float, and why and even how our continents float on the earth's mantle and move inch by inch over the ages.

Experiment 6.1

Can Water Exert an Upward Push?

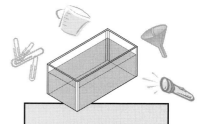

Materials

* ✳ fish tank or any other container filled with water
* ✳ small rock
* ✳ paper towel
* ✳ long rubber band about ¼ in wide
* ✳ ruler

In the previous chapter, it was shown that the pressure on an enclosed fluid is transmitted equally throughout the fluid. Does that mean water exerts an upward push on an object lowered into it? If the downward push is transmitted equally, how can water push any object upwards?

Lower a small rock to the bottom of the water. Does it rise back up? Remove the rock from the water and dry it.

Suspend the rock in a long rubber band and knot the rubber band to make a long loop supporting the rock (see Figure 22). Hold the rubber band at one end so that the rock hangs below. Observe how the rubber band stretches. Measure the stretched length with a ruler.

Repeat but this time let the rock hang so that it is underwater when you take the measurement. Compare the stretched lengths of the rubber band when the rock hangs in air and in water.

The stretched rubber band is shorter when the rock is in the water. This means that the rock weighs less in water. The water must be pushing the rock upward.

The deeper a spot is in the water, the greater is the weight of water above it, and as a result, as was shown in the previous

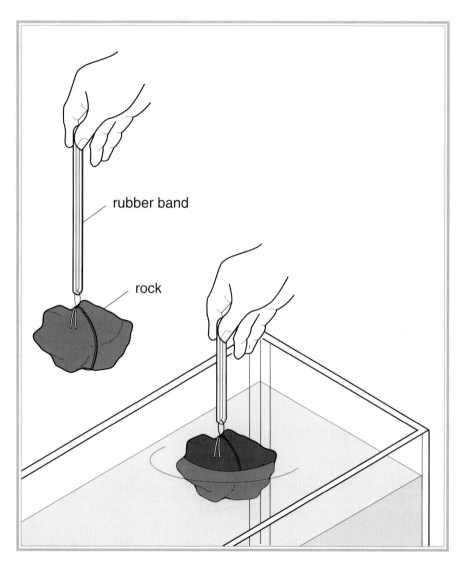

rubber band

rock

Figure 22. The weight of a rock can be supported by a rubber band in air and in water.

chapter, the greater is the pressure on that spot. But, at the bottom of an object in water, the pressure must be greater than at the top of the object. It is this *difference* in pressure that acts to push the object upward.

The force with which a fluid pushes an object upward in water is called the buoyant force. The buoyant force is due to the difference in pressure at the top and bottom of an object in the fluid.

The buoyant force makes it easier to lift anything within water compared to out of water. In this experiment, the buoyant force decreased the weight of the rock.

Experiment 6.2

Archimedes' Principle

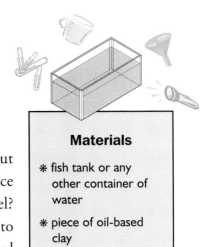

In Experiment 6.1, when you put the rock into water, did you notice what happened to the water level? The rock caused the water level to rise. It pushed water aside. A word for "pushing aside" is *displacement*. The rock displaces exactly its own volume of water. For example, if a rock is put into a jar of water that is filled to the top, the displaced water will flow over the top and can be caught in a basin below the jar. When measured, the water in the basin will have the same volume as the rock.

It was the displacement of water during his bath due to the volume of his body that led Archimedes to cry out "Eureka." He had discovered the principle of buoyancy. Archimedes' principle says that an object will sink until its weight equals the weight of the displaced water. The following experiment illustrates this.

Roll a one-inch cube of oil-based clay into a ball. Place it on the water. Does it float?

Change the shape by making the clay into a bowl with a thin flat bottom. Press on the sides of the clay bowl to make them as high and wide as possible. Place the clay bowl on the water. Does it float?

Change the weight. Fill the clay bowl with water. Does it float?

When the clay is shaped like a ball, it sinks. When shaped like a bowl, it floats. Does the clay change to some other substance? No. Has its weight changed? No. Only the shape of the clay changed. Why do you think the shape makes a difference?

The shape of the clay makes a difference because the shape determines how much water is displaced. According to Archimedes' principle, the force that pushes an object in water upward is equal to the weight of the displaced water. The more water displaced, the greater the upward (buoyant) force.

The weight of the object is a downward force. If the upward force (buoyant force) is greater than the downward force, the object floats. If the weight of the object is greater than the buoyant force, the object sinks.

Here is how Archimedes' principle worked for the ball and the bowl.

When the clay was shaped into a ball, it pushed aside the same-sized ball of water (see Figure 23a). The buoyant force equals the weight of the displaced water. The buoyant force was not as great as the weight of the clay ball. The clay ball sank.

When the clay was shaped like a bowl, it had a larger volume (see Figure 23b). As a result, it displaced more water than before. The buoyant force increased. The buoyant force became greater than the weight of the bowl. As a result, the clay bowl floated.

When the air in the bowl was replaced by water, the bowl weighed more. Its weight was greater than the weight of the displaced water (the buoyant force). The filled bowl sank.

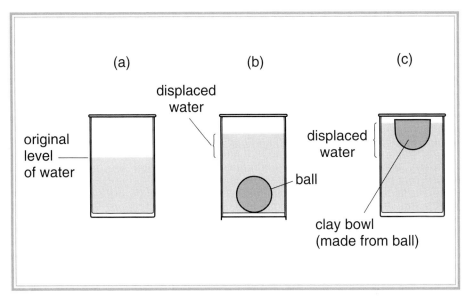

Figure 23. ARCHIMEDES' PRINCIPLE AND BUOYANT FORCE. a) Container of water at the start. b) The ball is submerged in water. The water level has gone up because it has been displaced by the ball. The weight of the displaced water equals the buoyant force on the ball. The weight of the ball (downward force) is greater than the buoyant force, so the ball sinks. c) Same container of water with clay now in shape of a stretched-out bowl. The water level is higher than in 23a because the clay bowl has a greater volume than the ball and so displaces more water than the ball. The weight of the displaced water equals the buoyant force on the bowl. This buoyant force is now greater than the weight (downward force) of the bowl. The clay bowl floats.

Submarines work by a process similar to that of the clay bowl with and without water in it. To cause it to sink, the ballast tanks of a submarine are filled with water. To rise, compressed air is released into the ballast tanks to push out the water.

Archimedes' principle was developed long before it was possible to make metal ships, but it was by applying Archimedes' principle that steamship engineers were first able to float metal ships. They designed them with air spaces so that they could float. In 1822, the *Aaron Manby* became the first iron ship to be successfully launched. Soon, most ships were built of iron. The *Titanic* sank because the air in the ship was replaced by the much heavier seawater gushing into it through the gashes in its side.

Project Ideas and Further Investigations

- Construct a toy submarine and use it to demonstrate Archimedes' principle. Plans for such devices may be found in science experiment books in libraries, or you can invent your own device. Use a diagram to illustrate how to make the submarine sink and float and explain why it works.
- Measure the buoyant force on a rock in two ways. The first way is to measure the weight of the water displaced by the rock. To find out the weight of the displaced water, consult physics or physical science experiment books on the overflow method, or invent your own method. The other way is similar to Experiment 6.1, but a spring scale, kitchen scale, or fish scale is used to measure the difference in weight between the rock in air and in water. Compare the results from the two methods and explain any differences.
- Hypothesize as to whether the buoyant force on a rock increases, decreases, or stays the same as the rock is lowered farther down into water. Test your hypothesis by measuring the buoyant force on a rock at different depths in water. **Under adult supervision**, try

measuring buoyancy in a swimming pool or lake. Repeat with a different kind of rock. What is the relationship between the buoyant force and the depth?

- Using the methods mentioned above to find weight and volume, apply Archimedes' principle to predict whether various objects will float or sink in water. Then, test your prediction by experiment.
- Test for the buoyancy of the same rock in water, salt water, corn syrup, and salad oil. Explain differences. You may want to try other liquids, too.
- How does temperature affect buoyancy in water?

Experiment 6.3

Density and Floating

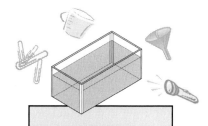

If you know the density of an object, you can immediately tell without any calculations whether or not it will sink in water.

Density is defined as the mass that occupies a specified volume of the material.

$$\text{Density} = \frac{\text{mass}}{\text{volume}}$$

One gram of water occupies one cubic centimeter of space, so the density of water is one gram per cubic centimeter. In common units, one square foot of water weighs 62.4 pounds.

Materials

* fish tank or any other large container filled with water

* samples of different materials such as ice cube, wood, candle, golf ball, Superball, unopened can of regular soda, unopened can of diet soda, glass marble or other chunk of glass, stainless steel fork, aluminum cup, small plastic bag filled with air and tied closed, small plastic bag filled with water and tied closed

According to Archimedes' principle, an object sinks if the weight of the water displaced by its volume is less than the weight of the object. Since weight is proportional to mass at the surface of the earth, an object sinks if its density is greater than that of water. It floats if its density is less than that of water.

Of the six pairs of items listed on the next page, which item in each pair is denser than water? Use the floating/sinking test for each one to find out.

The ice cube, Superball, can of diet soda, air-filled plastic bag, and candle will certainly float. The wood will probably

1. ice cube	small solid chunk of wood
2. golf ball	candle
3. Superball	glass marble or other small chunk of glass
4. unopened can of diet soda	stainless steel fork
5. unopened can of regular soda	aluminum measuring cup filled with water
6. small plastic bag filled with air and tied closed	small plastic bag filled with water (no air in the bag) and tied closed

float (the only wood that is denser than water is ebony). The bag filled with water will sink below the surface and float there. The golf ball, can of regular soda, glass, steel fork, and aluminum measuring cup filled with water will all sink.

The can of regular soda (metal container, water, flavor, sugar, air) sinks because it has enough sugar dissolved in it to make its overall density greater than that of water. The diet soda (metal container, water, flavor, artificial sweetener, air) has only a small weight of artificial sweetener, so its overall density remains less than that of water.

Project Idea and Further Investigation

Densities of different liquids may be measured by a hydrometer. A hydrometer is a narrow tube closed at one end and weighted to float upright in a liquid. The denser the liquid, the higher the tube floats. Commercially, such tubes are used to compare the density of water to battery acid, antifreeze, sugar solutions, and dairy milk. A hydrometer can be constructed from a piece of glass tubing open at both ends or even from a straw. Plug one end with oil-based clay so that the tube floats upright. Control how deep the hydrometer sinks by dropping brads or sand into it. Float the hydrometer in liquids of known density (stay away from antifreeze and battery acid and other poisonous or corrosive liquids) and place marks on the hydrometer to indicate how deep it sinks in each. These marks can be used to measure the densities of other solutions. Use the hydrometer to find the density of liquids other than water. It can also be used to find densities of solutions of different concentrations such as solutions of salt, sugar, or rubbing alcohol. A small test tube can be substituted for the tubing and a strip of paper can be placed inside it marked in millimeters to measure the floating height.

Experiment 6.4

What Determines How High an Object Floats?

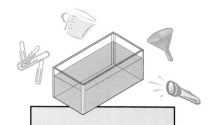

Materials

✳ fish tank or pail filled with water

✳ lightweight flat-bottomed plastic container, about one pint in size, with sides that are vertical or almost vertical, such as a small butter tub

✳ measuring cup

✳ ruler

✳ dry sand or pennies

According to Archimedes' principle, a floating object will sink in water until the weight of the water it displaces equals its own weight. Objects with low densities compared to that of water may descend only a little into the water. This is because only a little water needs to be displaced before its weight equals the weight of the low-density object. Objects with densities that are higher but still less than that of water will float lower in the water. The following experiment investigates this.

With the open end up, place a flat-bottomed, lightweight plastic container into the water. The container should have straight sides and float at or just below the surface.

Pour one half cup of water from a measuring cup into the floating container. With a ruler, measure the depth at which the bottom of the container has sunk. How do the levels of water inside and outside compare?

Add another half cup of water to the floating container. How do the levels of water inside and out compare now? Again, measure the depth to the bottom of the container.

Repeat the additions of water and measurements of depth until the container sinks. What do your measurements show?

Why does the container sink lower and lower as water is added? Does the container sink the same distance each time? Explain these results using Archimedes' principle.

Repeat the experiment but add measured half cups of sand or pennies to the container instead of water. How do the results differ? Does it take the same number of cups of sand or pennies as cups of water to sink the container?

When the first half cup of water is added, the container sinks until it displaces the same weight of water that has been added. At that level, according to Archimedes' principle, the downward and upward forces are equalized. The water levels inside and out are about equal.

When the water in the container is doubled, the process repeats. The container sinks down an additional depth equal to the one before. More water is displaced equal to that added. Water levels are equal inside and out. This process repeats until the top of the container sinks below the surface.

A half cup of sand weighs more than a half cup of water. When a half cup of sand is added to the container, it sinks into the water until the weight of the displaced water equals the weight of the sand. More than a half cup of water has to be displaced to equal the weight of the half cup of sand. The result is that the container sinks in more deeply. This continues as more sand is added. It takes fewer cups of sand than water to sink the container.

Ship captains must be careful to see that their ships are not overloaded or they will sink. In past centuries, such occurrences were not at all unusual. In England, at the urging of Samuel Plimsoll (1824–1898), a member of Parliament, the Merchant Shipping Act of 1875 became a law. This act established a reference line marking the loading limit for cargo ships. The Plimsoll line was adopted internationally in 1930. It indicates the maximum depth to which a ship can be safely loaded. You may have seen Plimsoll lines on the side of ships. Usually, there are not one but four to six lines. This is because the densities of fresh water, salt water, cold water, and warm water are different. A ship will float the lowest in warm fresh water and the highest in cold salt water.

Project Ideas and Further Investigations

- Use the method of Experiment 6.3 to find and compare the densities of other materials with that of water. Note that this may depend upon whether or not there are pockets of air in the substance as in, for example, all powdered solids. Use Archimedes' principle and explain the various results.
- Make a square block of ice. Float it in water. Find out how much of the ice is below the water. Determine the density of ice from this information. Why does the density of ice make icebergs so dangerous to shipping?
- Does a tangerine float? Does an orange float? Find out. Do they float after peeling? If either sinks after peeling, take measurements to find out why. Find out whether other fruits float or sink. Does a peanut float? Investigate other foods, too. Explain your observations.

- What is the weight needed to push a Ping-Pong ball underwater? Is this weight equal to the buoyant force on the ball? Explain.
- Use a toy boat or make one from a tin can. Allow a reasonable clearance at the top for safety if the water were to become disturbed. Experiment to find Plimsoll lines for the boat in hot water, cold water, cold seawater, and warm seawater. Create a chart with diagrams that explain these lines.

Experiment 6.5

How Do Fish Float?

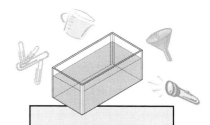

Materials

* fish tank or other container filled with water

* small lump of protein in the form of cheese

* small thin resealable plastic bag

* 100 mL graduated cylinder or kitchen measuring cup

* laboratory balance or kitchen scale

* container or sink filled with salt water

Think of what an advantage the ability to float gives to a fish! Instead of using most of its energy just to stay afloat, the fish can put the same energy into other actions. How does a fish manage to float despite the fact that, as a whole, a fish is slightly denser than water?

Sharks, rays, mackerel, blennies, and flatfishes have not developed a way to float. They have to swim all the time to avoid sinking.

A fish that can float in water is different in that it possesses a swim bladder. A swim bladder is a sack in the upper half of a fish that is filled with gas. If more gas is added to the swim bladder, the fish becomes less dense and can float higher up. If gas is somehow removed from the swim bladder, the fish becomes more dense and sinks lower. This is similar to the way a submarine uses density differences to move up and down in the water. Many fish can suck air in at the surface to decrease density and can "burp" the air out to decrease buoyancy. Other fish can develop gas for the swim bladder with a gas gland. Such fish give off oxygen into the swim bladder or reabsorb the oxygen into their blood so as to alter their volume and buoyancy.

Since water pressure increases with depth, the gas in the swim bladder is compressed as the fish descends in water. The fish must add gas to the swim bladder to stay at that depth. As the fish ascends, the pressure on the gas in the swim bladder decreases. The fish must deflate the swim bladder to avoid soaring to the surface.

Some fish have sealed bladders and cannot burp out the gas. They have to be careful not to rise too quickly. If they do, the decreasing water pressure can cause the swim bladder to expand so that it might burst. The fish has to rise slowly and use its swimming fins while reabsorbing the gas.

To roughly examine the idea of the swim bladder, try the following experiment.

Place a small lump of protein tissue (cheese) into a thin resealable plastic bag. Carefully press air out of the bag and seal it tight. The bag should not be inflated by any trapped air. The package of wrapped protein simulates a fish with a swim bladder. Weigh the package.

Place the package in a fish tank. Does it sink or float? Place the package into a measuring cup or graduated cylinder partly filled with water and measure its volume from the difference in water levels before and after the addition of the package.

Remove the package and admit a little air into it. Reseal. Does it float? Continue adding air and sealing until the bag floats. This now simulates a fish with an expanded swim bladder. Measure the volume of the sealed bag. Weigh it.

At this point, you know the starting weight of the protein and the weight with enough air added for it to float. What percent of the total volume of the package must be air for the protein to float in fresh water?

Repeat the experiment but use salt water instead of fresh water. What percent of the total volume of the package must be air for the fish to float in salt water?

Freshwater fish need larger swim bladders than saltwater fish because salt water is denser than fresh water. Calculations show that a freshwater fish needs a bladder of air to fill 7 percent of its body volume in order to stay afloat, but a saltwater fish needs only 5 percent.

Inhaling air helps a person to float in water. When a human inhales, the chest cavity expands. The body's volume increases with only a very slight increase in weight. This results in a decrease in body density. It is this decrease that helps a person to float.

The Dead Sea in Israel is very dense because it has a very high salt content. It is easy to float in the water there. People have been observed reading a book while comfortably floating on their backs.

Divers who work underwater need to achieve "neutral buoyancy." That is, they need to neither sink nor rise. The buoyancy of a diver depends on a number of things such as the amount of body fat, the weight and type of dive suit and air tank, and the weight of the equipment carried. A diver who is liable to float to the surface may need to use a weight belt to increase body density. If the diver is too heavy, a device to which air can be added as needed to decrease the density of the diver can be used.

Project Ideas and Further Investigations

Whenever working with uncooked animal tissue, whether fat or protein, wear plastic gloves and be sure to wash your hands and tools thoroughly when the work is completed.

- Is it true that people with fat on their bodies can float more easily than lean people? Conduct an experiment (as in Experiment 6.5) to test this. You can simulate fat tissues with strips of animal fat and lean muscle with strips of lean meat.
- How does a life preserver work? How can a ship-wrecked person convert a shirt into water wings? Devise demonstrations to show how these work.
- Look in physics experiment books to find out what a Cartesian diver is. Make one of your own.
- Determine the density of a live fish from your fish tank. To do this without endangering the fish, be sure that it is in tank water the entire time.
- Visit a local fish market and obtain samples of tissues of fish of different species, preferably both saltwater and freshwater fish. Weigh them and measure the volumes. How do the densities compare? Which species would float only in salt water but not in fresh water? **Wash your hands with warm water and soap after handling any raw fish.**

Further Reading

Bloomfield, Louis A. *How Things Work.* New York: John Wiley & Sons, Inc.,1997.

Ehrlich, Robert. *Turning the World Inside Out and 174 Other Simple Physics Demonstrations.* Princeton, N.J.: Princeton University Press, 1990.

———. *Why Toast Lands Jelly-Side Down.* Princeton, N.J.: Princeton University Press, 1997.

Gardner, Robert. *Experimenting with Water.* New York: Franklin Watts, Inc., 1993.

———. *Science Projects About Physics in the Home.* Springfield, N.J.: Enslow Publishers, Inc., 1999.

Hewitt, Paul G. *Conceptual Physical Science.* Menlo Park, Calif.: Addison Wesley Longman, Inc., 1999.

Martin, Lawrence. *Scuba Diving Explained.* Flagstaff, Ariz.: Best Publishing Co., 1997.

Rybolt, Thomas, and Robert C. Mebane. *Environmental Experiments about Water.* Hillside, N.J.: Enslow Publishers, Inc., 1993.

Internet Addresses

Argonne National Laboratory. *Newton BBS.*
<http://www.newton.dep.anl.gov/>

The Exploratorium. <http://www.exploratorium.edu/>

Kiselev, Sergey, and Tanya Yanovsky-Kiselev. *Total Internal Reflection.* © 1997.
<http://www.lightlink.com/sergey/java/java/totintrefl>

Science and Mathematics Initiative for Learning Enhancement. *SMILE Program Physics Index.*
<http://www.iit.edu/~smile/physinde.html>

ThinkQuest Library. *Discovering Light.* © 1999.
<http://library.thinkquest.org/27356/>

University of Maryland Physics Lecture-Demonstration Facility. *Demonstration List by Outline Topic.*
<http://www.physics.umd.edu/deptinfo/facilities/lecdem/demolst.htm#c2>

The University of North Carolina at Wilmington. *Aquarius— The World's Only Underwater Laboratory.* "The Physics of Underwater Diving." <http://www.uncwil.edu/nurc/aquarius/lessons/buoyancy.htm>

Washington State University. *Mad Sci Network.* © 1995–2000. <http://www.madsci.org>

Index

Science Projects

About the

Human Body

Robert Gardner

ENSLOW PUBLISHERS, INC.

Bloy St. & Ramsey Ave.	P.O. Box 38
Box 777	Aldershot
Hillside, NJ 07205	Hants GU12 6BP
U.S.A.	U.K.

Library of Congress Cataloging-in-Publication Data

Gardner, Robert, 1929–
    Science projects about the human body/Robert Gardner.
        p. cm.
    Includes bibliographical references and index.
    Summary: Includes suggestions for projects about various aspects
of the human body.
    ISBN 0-89490-443-4
    1. Human physiology—Juvenile literature. 2. Body, Human—
Juvenile literature. 3. Science projects—Juvenile literature.
[1. Body, Human. 2. Science projects.] 1. Title.
QP37.G36 1993
612'.0078—dc20   92-43802
                                                          CIP
                                                           AC

Printed in the United States of America

10 9 8 7 6 5 4 3 2 1

Illustration Credits: Jacob Katari

Cover Photo: David Young-Wolff/Photo Edit

Contents

*appropriate for science fair project ideas

*appropriate for science fair project ideas

Introduction

The science projects and experiments in this book have to do with people. You will need a friend to help you with many of the experiments. You'll be asking other friends and family members to serve as subjects in a variety of experiments or surveys. Since some of the experiments will take some time, try to choose friends who are patient. It might be best if you could work with others who enjoy experimenting with people as much as you do. In that way, you could take turns being experimenters and subjects.

As you do these projects, you will find it useful to record your ideas, notes, data, and anything you can conclude from your experiments in a notebook so you can keep track of the information you gather and the conclusions you reach. It will allow you to refer back to other experiments you have done that may be useful to you in projects you'll do later.

Science Fairs

Some of the projects in this book might be appropriate for a science fair. Those projects are marked with an asterisk (*). However, judges at such fairs do not reward projects or experiments that are simply copied from a book. For example, a model of the human eye, which is commonly found at these fairs, would probably not impress judges unless it was done in a novel or creative way. A model of the eye with a flexible lens that could produce images of objects at any distance from the "eye" would receive more consideration than a rigid papier-mâché model.

Science fair judges tend to reward creative thought and imagination. However, it is difficult to be creative or imaginative unless you are really interested in your project, so choose something that appeals to you. Consider, too, your own ability and the cost of materials needed for the project.

If you decide to use a project found in this book for a science fair, you will need to find ways to modify or extend the project. This should not be difficult because you will probably find that, as you do these projects, new ideas for experiments will come to mind. These new experiments could make excellent science fair projects, particularly because they spring from your own mind and are interesting to you.

If you decide to enter a science fair and have never done so before, you should read some of the books listed in the Bibliography. The references that deal specifically with science fairs will provide plenty of helpful hints and lots of useful information that will enable you to avoid the pitfalls that sometimes plague first-time entrants. You'll learn how to prepare appealing reports that include charts and graphs, how to set up and display your work, how to present your project, and how to relate to judges and visitors.

Safety First

Most of the projects included in this book are perfectly safe. However, some contain warnings that should be carefully observed. The following safety rules are well worth reading before you start any project:

1. Do any experiments or projects, whether from this book or of your own design, under the supervision of a science teacher or other knowledgeable adult.

2. Read all instructions carefully before proceeding with a project. If you have questions, check with your supervisor before going any further.

3. Maintain a serious attitude while conducting experiments. Fooling around can be dangerous to you and to others.

4. Wear approved safety goggles when you are doing anything that might cause injury to your eyes.

5. Do not eat or drink while experimenting.

6. Have a first aid kit nearby while you are experimenting.

7. Do not put your fingers or any object in electrical outlets.

8. Never experiment with household electricity except under the supervision of a knowledgeable adult.

9. Don't touch a lit high-wattage bulb. Light bulbs produce light, but they also produce heat.

10. Never look directly at the sun. It can cause permanent damage to your eyes.

1

Your Beating Heart

Deep within your chest, your heart does not skip a beat as it pumps blood to all parts of your body. Like any pump, it raises the pressure of the liquid it pushes along. Your doctor has probably measured the pressure of your blood as it flows through the artery in your arm. Some of the arteries coming out of your heart carry blood to the lungs. There the oxygen in the air you breathe is absorbed by your blood. And it's in these same lungs that the waste gases carried by your blood are transmitted to the air.

In this chapter, you will have a chance to investigate the workings of the hearts and lungs of a number of people, including yourself. You will learn what factors make your heart beat faster or slower. You will find out what makes us change the rate at which we breathe, how much air we breathe with every breath, and how our breathing rates and heart rates compare with those of other animals. You will find out how we breathe, how to take a person's pulse, how to find the valves in your veins, and many other things about the hearts, blood vessels, and lungs inside people.

YOUR WORKING HEART

Usually, you are not aware that your heart is beating. But once in a while, after you've been running or if you are frightened, you may feel your heart pounding inside your chest.

The average person's heart, which is roughly the size of his or her fist, beats about 70 times each minute. With each beat, your heart contracts and squeezes about 60 milliliters (ml) or 2 ounces (oz) of blood into your arteries.

Things you'll need:

- small rubber ball
- clock or watch with second hand or second mode
- stethoscope or cardboard mailing or tube from a paper towel roll
- kitchen funnel

To get some idea of how much work your heart does, try this. Hold a rubber ball in your hand. Pretend your hand is your heart and the rubber ball is the blood inside your heart. Squeeze the ball at a steady rate of about 70 times every minute.

How does your hand feel after you've been squeezing for several minutes? Do you think your heart does very much work in a day? The energy for the muscle cells in your heart comes from the food carried to them by blood. Do you see why it is essential that the flow of blood to the heart not be interrupted?

Ask a friend if you can listen to his or her heart. If you have a stethoscope, place it several inches above and slightly to the left (your friend's left) of the lower end of his or her breast bone (sternum). If you don't have a stethoscope, put your ear there. Listen to the two distinct sounds that occur with each beat—lub-dub, lub-dub . . . Can your friend hear your heart beat? Can you hear the sounds better if you place a short length of cardboard tube on your friend's chest? Does it help if you place a small kitchen funnel at the end of the tube near the chest? Can you find other ways to improve a homemade stethoscope?

TAKE YOUR PULSE*

Every time your heart beats, it forces blood into the arteries that lead from your heart to the millions of cells that make up your body.

Things you'll need:
- small piece of clay
- soda straw

When the blood enters your elastic arteries, they expand to accept the added fluid. Then, as the heart relaxes, the arteries contract like a stretched rubber band when it is released. A wave of expansion and contraction moves along the arteries with each heartbeat. In those places where the arteries are near the surface of your body, you can feel this wave. It is called a pulse. When a doctor or a nurse takes your pulse, he or she can feel the wave that moves along the artery in your wrist.

The pulse on the lower side of your wrist is just a short distance behind the point where your thumb connects with your wrist. Figure 1 shows you the approximate position where this pulse can be felt. To feel a pulse, place your two middle fingers on the underside of your or someone else's wrist. Do not use your thumb because it has a pulse too.

Other places where a pulse can be felt easily are at the temple, just in front of the ear, and on the throat at either side of the Adam's apple. Can you find these pulse points? Can you find other pulse points on your body, such as the inside of your biceps (upper arm) muscle? How many can you find?

With a simple amplifying device, you can even *see* the pulse in your wrist. Place your hand with your palm turned upward on a table or counter. Put a small lump of clay above the pulse point on your wrist or on a friend's wrist. Then stick a soda straw upright in the clay. Watch the soda straw. What happens to it each time an expansion-contraction wave moves along the radial artery (the artery that lies near the inner surface of the wrist)? Can you use this amplifier to detect other pulse points in the body?

10

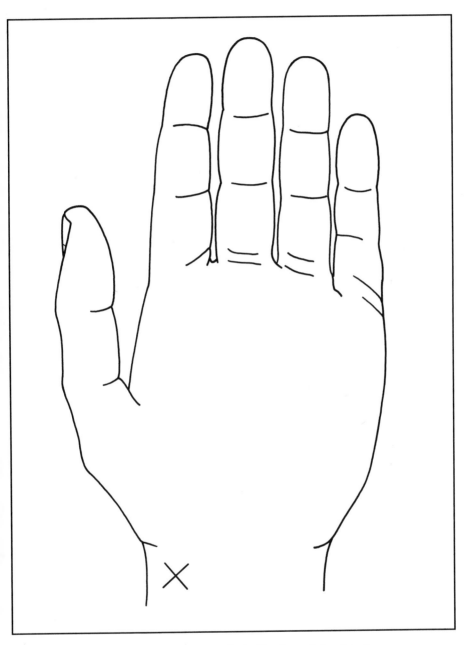

Figure 1: The X marks the place on the inside of your left wrist where you can feel a pulse

CHANGING HEART RATES*

Normally your heart beats about 70 times each minute, but what happens when you exercise? When you lie down? When you grow older?

Things you'll need:
- clock or watch with a second hand or second mode

Ask a friend to lie down and relax. After a few minutes, measure your friend's pulse rate, that is, the number of pulse waves each minute. Record your results in your notebook. Remember, a pulse wave moves along the arteries every time the heart beats. The number of pulse waves each minute is equal to the number of times your friend's heart beats in one minute. To avoid any effects due to exercise or body position, all your measurements should be made after the person has been lying quietly for at least five minutes and at least an hour after any vigorous exercise.

Ask your friend to sit up. After a few minutes, measure and record his or her heart rate again. Then measure your friend's heart rate after he or she has been standing for five minutes. Try this experiment on several different people.

Does the position of a person's body (lying, sitting, standing) affect his or her heart rate? If so, how is heart rate related to body position?

Measure and record a friend's heart rate after he or she hops twenty times on one leg. After hopping fifty times on one leg. After running a race. Repeat the experiment on a number of people.

How does exercise affect a person's heart rate?

What do you think happens to your friend's heart rate when he or she is asleep? With permission, measure your friend's heart rate while he or she is asleep. Was your prediction correct?

Are people's heart rates related to their age? To find out, measure and record the heart rates of as many different people as possible. Measure the heart rates of babies, young children, teenagers, young adults, middle-aged people, and elderly people. Examine your results carefully. Does age appear to affect a person's heart rate? If so, how is age related to heart rate?

Table 1 gives the heart rates for a number of different mammals and birds. How does the value for a human's heart rate given in the table compare with the one you obtained?

Does the heart rate of mammals appear to be related to their size? How about birds? If there is a relationship, how does the heart rate change as the size of the animal increases? If you have a dog, determine his or her hear rate by placing your ear against the dog's chest. Is the dog's heart rate more or less than yours?

Design an experiment to find out whether the heart rates of boys and girls are the same or different. How many different people do you think you should test?

ANIMAL	HEART RATE†	ANIMAL	HEART RATE†
MAMMALS		mouse	376
at	660	seal	80
at (hibernating)	30	shrew	800
amel	28	white rat	300
at	200	**BIRDS**	
ow	50	crow	380
lephant	30	hummingbird	1200
iraffe	66	mallard	320
oat	81	ostrich	65
rey whale	9	robin	570
edgehog	250	sparrow	50
uman	70	starling	390
ion	40	turkey	93

Table 1: The heart rates of various animals.

†Heart rate of animal at rest (beats per minute)

WATCHING YOUR BLOOD FLOW*

Each time your heart beats it pumps blood into your arteries. This causes the pressure of the blood in these vessels to increase. Between heartbeats, when your heart muscle is relaxing, the blood pressure drops. Because arteries are elastic, they stretch when the heart forces blood into them, and they contract when the heart relaxes. The valves between the heart and the arteries that lead from the heart allow blood to flow in only one direction. As a result, the blood in the arteries continues to be pushed outward away from the heart even when the heart is relaxing. The valves prevent the contracting arteries from pushing blood back into the heart.

Blood travels away from the heart through arteries. The arteries lead into smaller vessels called arterioles. Beyond the arterioles lie very tiny vessels called capillaries. These vessels are so thin that chemicals can move through their walls. It is through these vessels that the cells of your body receive food from the blood and transfer waste products to the blood.

After passing through the capillaries, the blood begins its journey back to the heart. The vessels that carry blood to the heart are called veins. The pressure in these vessels is much less than it is in the arteries. In fact, without muscular contractions that squeeze the veins, blood tends to collect in the veins of the lower body. To prevent blood from draining into the legs instead of moving toward the heart, veins contain valves. These valves allow blood to flow only one way—toward the heart.

You can see the location of some of these valves quite easily. Because many veins lie near the surface of the body, you can see them through the skin. They have a bluish tint. In fact, they sometimes bulge above the skin on the back of the hand or the forearm. If you have difficulty seeing such a vessel, let your arm hang down for a few moments so that more blood will collect in the veins.

Once you can see your veins clearly, hold your thumb on a vein near its lower end. This will seal off the vein. For example, you might put your thumb on one of the veins in your forearm. Then "sweep" the blood in the vein toward the heart by moving your index finger a short distance along the vein. Gradually increase the distance you move your finger. When you reach a valve, the vein below the valve will collapse and become difficult to see when you lift your finger. You'll be able to see the blood-filled vein above the valve but not below it. Can you then locate the next valve along the vein?

Hold one hand over your head for 20 seconds. Let the other one hang at your side. Then look at the back of both hands. One hand is redder than the other. Which one is it? Why is one hand redder than the other?

BREATHING RATE (SUPPLYING OXYGEN FOR YOUR BLOOD)*

Your beating heart pumps blood that brings oxygen and food to the cells of your body. In an earlier project, you saw that the rate that your heart

Things you'll need:
- clock or watch with a second hand or second mode

beats changes with age and exercise. To get oxygen into your blood, you have to draw air into your lungs. It is inside the lungs that your blood comes into close contact with the oxygen in the air.

A person's breathing rate is the number of times he or she inhales (draws air into the lungs) and exhales (pushes air out of the lungs) in one minute. Do you think your breathing rate changes with age and exercise? How do you think your breathing rate compares with your heart rate? To find out, ask a friend to lie quietly on his or her back. After a few minutes, determine your friend's breathing rate. You can do this by watching his or her chest move up and down. Or, by listening closely, you can hear the air moving in and out of his or her nose. Measure the rate several times to be sure your friend's breathing rate is constant. How many times does your friend breathe in one minute?

To avoid any effects due to exercise or body position, all your measurements should be recorded after the person has been lying quietly for at least five minutes and at least an hour after any vigorous exercise.

Ask your friend to sit up. After a few minutes measure and record his or her breathing rate again. Then measure your friend's breathing rate after he or she has been standing for five minutes. Repeat the experiment on several different people.

Does the position of a person's body (lying, sitting, standing) affect his or her breathing rate? If so, how is breathing rate related to body position?

Measure and record your friend's breathing rate after he or she hops twenty times on one leg. After hopping fifty times on one leg.

After running a race. If possible, repeat this experiment with a number of different people. How does exercise affect a person's breathing rate?

What do you think happens to your friend's breathing rate when he or she is asleep? With permission, measure your friend's breathing rate while he or she is asleep. Was your prediction correct?

Is a person's breathing rate related to his or her age? To find out, you can measure and record the breathing rates of as many different people as possible. You will need to measure the breathing rates of babies, young children, teenagers, young adults, middle-aged people, and elderly people. Examine your results carefully. Does age appear to affect a person's breathing rate? If so, how is breathing rate related to age?

How does your breathing rate compare with that of your dog or cat? If possible, compare the breathing rates of other animals. Table 2 shows some breathing rates for a number of different animals.

Is the breathing rate for a human given in the table similar to the value you obtained? Does the size of an animal appear to affect its breathing rate? If so, how?

ANIMAL	BREATHING RATE†	ANIMAL	BREATHING RATE†
beaver	16	horse	10
blue whale	4	human	12
chipmunk	65	rabbit	37
deer mouse	135	rat	86
giraffe	32	Rhesus monkey	33
goat	19	sheep	20
guinea pig	90	shrew	190

Table 2: The breathing rate of various animals while at rest.
†Breathing rate of animal at rest (breaths per minute)

HOW MUCH AIR DO YOU BREATHE?*

How much air do you breathe each day? One way to find out is to measure the volume of air you breathe in and out in one normal breath. To do this you will need a plastic container. It should be big enough for you to put both your fists into it easily. Empty the container and place a piece of masking tape along its side as shown in Figure 2a. Using the measuring cup, pour a pint (2 cups, 470 ml) of water into the container. Use the marking pen to make a line at the level of the water in the container. Continue adding pints of water and making marks until the container is nearly full.

Things you'll need:

- large plastic container (about one gallon in size) that allows you to see the water level inside
- masking tape
- measuring cup
- marking pen
- small plastic bag (6-inch x 8-inch) and twist-tie
- one-gallon plastic milk container
- large pan, such as a dishpan
- piece of rubber or plastic tubing

To begin the experiment, have the container filled to about the 4-pint (8 cups, 1900 ml) level. Record the level of the water. You will need this information later. Flatten a small (6-inch x 8-inch) plastic bag so that it contains no air. *Do not use a larger size bag.* When you are breathing at your normal rate, hold your nose so that all the air you breathe passes through your mouth. After breathing this way for a short time, place the open end of the plastic bag firmly against and around your mouth just before you exhale. Collect the exhaled air in the bag. Immediately after you finish exhaling, twist the open end of the bag to seal off the air you breathed into it. Tie off the neck of the bag with a twist-tie. The bag now contains the air you exhaled in one breath.

To find out how much air you exhaled, hold the bag in your hand and push it under the water in the container. When the water rises, mark the new level of the water in the container. Make another mark

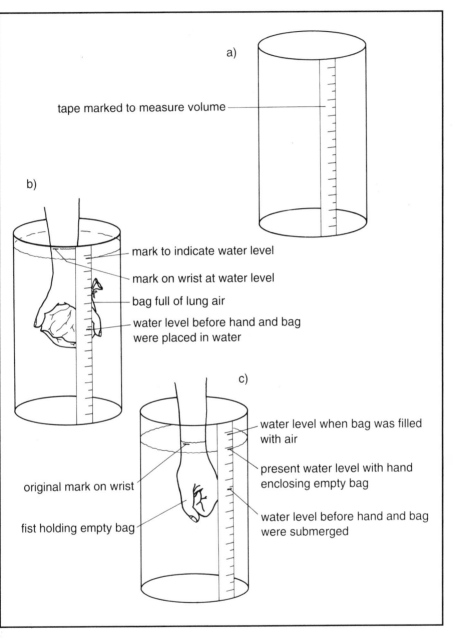

Figure 2: An experiment to measure the volume of air in one breath

on your wrist at the point where it touches the water. (See Figure 2b). Remove the bag from the water. Now force all the air out of the bag, hold it in your fist, and push your hand into the water until it reaches the mark on your wrist. Mark the water level in the container again (Figure 2c). From the orginal water level in the container and the two marks you have made you should be able to figure out how much air you exhaled in one breath.

Based on the volume of one breath and your breathing rate, what volume of air do you breathe in one day? In one year? Since a pint of air weighs about 0.57 grams, what weight of air do you breathe in one day? In one year?

To find out what volume of air you breathe when you take a deep breath, try an experiment with a one-gallon plastic milk container. A piece of tape along the side of the jug can be used to mark the water level. Fill the container with water, put the cap on, and invert the water-filled container in the pan of water. Remove the cap and insert one end of the rubber or plastic tubing into the mouth of the container as shown in Figure 3. *Do not inhale through the tube!* Have a friend hold the container so it does not squeeze the tubing. After taking a deep breath, exhale through the tube into the water-filled jug. The air you exhale will replace some of the water in the container. As soon as you stop exhaling, squeeze the end of the tube near your mouth and remove the tube from the container. Mark the water level in the jug. How much water does it take to fill the container to the mark you made? What volume of air did you breathe into the jug?

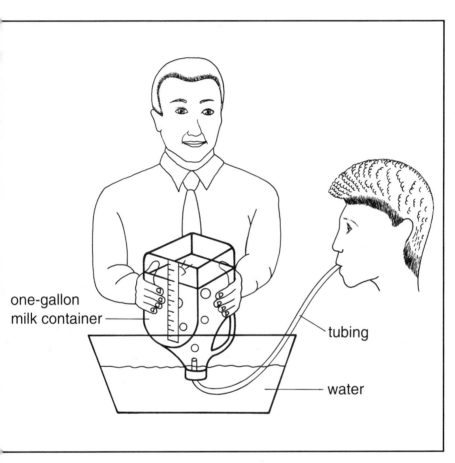

one-gallon
milk container

tubing

water

Figure 3: Another way to measure the volume of one breath

HOW WE BREATHE

Use your hands to feel what happens to your abdomen and chest when you inhale. You will find that your abdomen is pushed out. That is because your diaphragm, which separates your chest from your abdomen, moves downward and pushes on your stomach and the other organs in your abdomen. At the same time, the muscles in your chest contract, lifting your ribs upward and outward. The result of these movements is to increase the size of your chest. This, in turn, reduces the pressure of the air in your lungs, which fill much of your chest. Since the pressure of the air outside your body is now greater than the pressure inside, air is forced into your lungs. When you exhale, just the opposite happens. The rib cage falls; the diaphragm rises; the pressure in your lungs increases; and air is forced out of your lungs.

Things you'll need:

- glass or plastic tube
- rubber stopper, cork, or modeling clay
- large, clear, plastic bottle
- balloon
- rubber bands
- large cut-off balloon or rubber dam sheet such as dentists use

A model that illustrates the way we draw air into our lungs is shown in Figure 4. You can make such a model quite easily. *Ask an adult to help you cut off the bottom of the clear plastic bottle. Ask the same adult to insert a glass or plastic tube through a one-hole rubber stopper or cork, or modeling clay.* The stopper, cork, or clay is inserted in the mouth of the bottle as shown in the drawing. The tube represents the trachea—the tube that connects your lungs with your mouth. What does the rubber dam fixed to the bottom of the bottle represent? What does the balloon represent? What happens to the balloon when you pull down on the "diaphragm"? Why does it happen? What happens when you release it? Why?

The model you've built has nothing to represent the rib cage or anything to show why our lungs don't collapse every time our diaphragm muscle relaxes. Can you build a model that better illustrates the real breathing process?

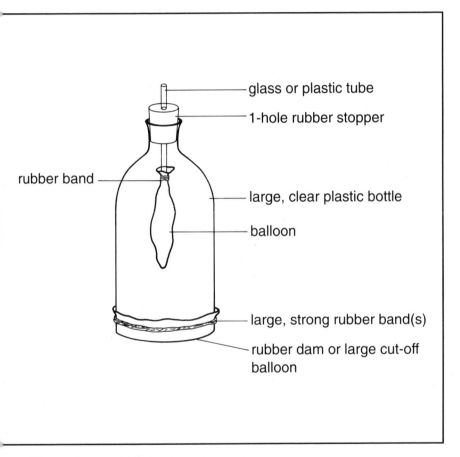

Figure 4: A model to show how a lung works

2

Come to Your Senses

You know about the world around you because you have sense organs. These organs make you aware that you are touching something or something is touching you. They enable you to feel heat and cold, pressure, and pain. You can taste and smell food. You can hear sounds and see objects that emit and reflect light. Nerve impulses from these sense organs travel to your brain where you become conscious of the heat, cold, pain, pressure, sound, or whatever. It is in the brain too, that other nerve impulses are established that allow you to respond to the sensations you perceive. You pull your hand away from a hot object. You duck when a baseball comes at your head. You speak in response to words you have heard, and you put on a coat when the air feels cold.

In this chapter, you will learn how to locate and map the various sensory receptors in your skin. You will find out where the receptors for various tastes are located on your tongue. You will experiment with sound and hearing, and you will find that your senses can sometimes be fooled. The very important sense of sight will be the subject of Chapter 3.

SENSES IN THE SKIN*

Your eye is the only organ that has nerve receptors that respond to light, and the nerve fibers in your ear enable you to hear. However, there are other nerve fibers in the skin all over your body. Some of these nerve cells respond to touch, some to pain, some to heat, and others to cold. Still others, which are located a little deeper in the skin, respond to pressure. A fly landing on your arm might stimulate touch receptor cells. A handshake would bend the skin in your hand and stimulate nerve receptor cells that respond to pressure.

Things you'll need:

- straight pins
- flat eraser
- fine-tipped felt pen
- ruler
- dull pencil
- paper clip or finishing nail
- ice cube
- glove
- 4-inch-long steel nail
- hot water in an insulated cup
- paper towel

Touch Receptors

As you might guess, there are lots of touch receptors in the skin on your fingertips. Even if you touch a fingertip very lightly, you can feel it. But are they as close together in other places on your body? You can find out by making a simple touch tester. Push two straight pins into a flat eraser as shown in Figure 5.

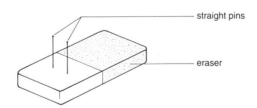

straight pins

eraser

Figure 5: A simple touch tester

To begin, set the heads of the pins about one-quarter inch or one-half centimeter apart. Ask a friend to close his or her eyes. Then touch the two pins to one of your friend's fingertips. Ask your friend to tell you whether he or she feels one or two points touching the skin. Repeat the experiment on other fingertips, the palm of the hand, the back of the hand, different parts of the arm, the lips, ears, neck, and back. Touch the pins to the skin in several places in each area you test. *Do not put the pins near anyone's eyes.*

Now set the two pins about half an inch or one centimeter apart and repeat the experiment. Can your friend now detect two touch points in regions that were reported as a single point before? Try the experiment again with the pin heads one inch or two centimeters apart. If possible do the same experiment on a number of different people.

Which parts of the body's skin appear to have the greatest number of touch receptors per area? Which parts have the least?

Sometimes touch receptors are located at the base of hairs. If you use a pencil to move single hairs on your friend's arm, can he or she detect the touch? Do all these hairs appear to have touch receptors near them? How about other hairs, such as those located on the head or the back of the neck?

When Touch Receptors Fail

Sometimes your touch receptors can be fooled. Pinch a pencil between the tips of your index and middle fingers. How many pencils do you feel? Now cross the same index and middle fingers. Pull your middle finger over your index finger. Place the same pencil between these fingertips again. How many pencils do you feel now?

Pain Receptors

Use a fine felt-tipped pen and a ruler to draw a grid like the one shown in Figure 6 on the back of a friend's hand. Draw a similar grid in your

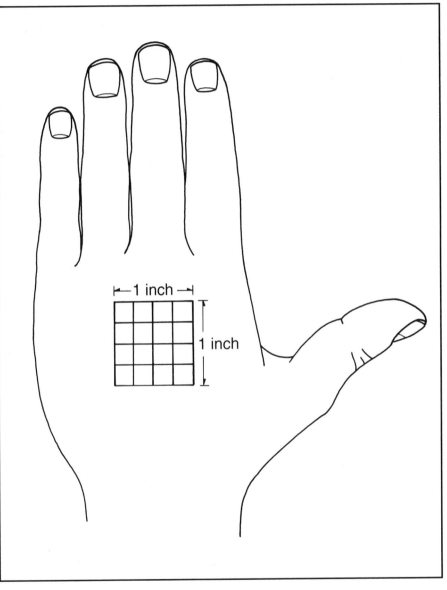

Figure 6: A grid you can use for locating pain receptors

notebook. Ask your friend to close his or her eyes. Use the point of a straight pin to touch each box in the grid on the skin. Touch the skin carefully. Each time you bring the pin to the grid, ask your friend if he or she feels any pain. If the answer is yes, make a check mark in that position in the grid in your notebook. If the answer is no, leave that position in the grid empty.

In how many of the sixteen grid positions did your friend feel pain? About how far apart are the pain receptors on the back of your friend's hand?

Repeat the experiment for other parts of your friend's skin. You might try the palm of the hand, both sides of the forearm and upper arm, the neck, the back, the foot, and the front and back of the lower leg.

Pressure Receptors

Repeat the experiment you did for pain receptors, but this time use a dull pencil to search for receptors that respond to pressure. What do you find about the distribution of pressure receptors in the skin?

Temperature Receptors

There are receptors for hot and cold in your skin. You can map the cold receptors on a grid as you have done before. The positions within the grid can be touched with the end of a partially unfolded paper clip or a finishing nail that is held firmly against an ice cube as shown in Figure 7. Wrapping the ice in a paper towel or a cloth will prevent meltwater from dripping onto your friend's skin. As you probably know, a long wire loses or gains heat very rapidly, so be sure the end of the paper clip or nail that is used to touch skin does not extend very far from the ice. If you wear a glove, you can comfortably hold the paper clip firmly against the ice.

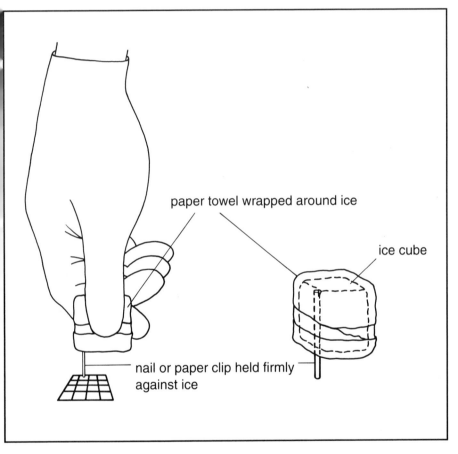

paper towel wrapped around ice

ice cube

nail or paper clip held firmly against ice

Figure 7: A device for locating nerve receptors sensitive to cold

Begin by touching the cold metal to grid points on the back of your friend's hand. Which grid positions contain cold receptors?

Again, try the experiment on various parts of your friend's body. Where on the skin are cold receptors most abundant? Where are they least likely to be found?

To test for receptors that respond to heat, *ask an adult to pour hot water from a teakettle into an insulated cup near a sink. Put on a glove and hold the head of a 4-inch nail. Place the nail, sharp-end first, into the hot water.* Quickly wipe off any hot water with a paper towel and use the narrow tip of the nail to search along grids for receptors that respond to heat. You will have to put the nail back into the hot water every few seconds because it will cool off rapidly.

A somewhat less-refined search for heat receptors can be done using an eyedropper that has a fine tip. Fill an insulated cup with water as hot as you can get it from the hot water faucet. *Do not use boiling water.* Put the eyedropper in the water and fill it. Then use the eyedropper to squeeze tiny drops of the hot water onto the back of your friend's hand. Refill the eyedropper frequently because the water will cool quickly in the eyedropper.

Where on the body are heat receptors most abundant? Where are they least abundant? About how far apart are the heat receptors on the back of your friend's hand? How far apart are they on his or her palm? Arm? Back? Lips?

TONGUES ARE FOR TALKING AND TASTING*

When you are talking you probably are not conscious of what your tongue is doing. So reread the last sentence aloud, but this time pay attention to all the movements your tongue makes. Now wash your hands and then hold your tongue so it cannot move. Try to read the sentence aloud once more.

Of course, you also move other muscles when you talk. Read the sentence once more without moving your lips. And again without moving your jaw. You can do this by keeping your teeth together as you speak. Which seems most essential to speech: tongue, lips, or jaw?

Things you'll need:

- cotton swabs
- small glasses, vials, or medicine cups to hold liquids
- salt
- water
- artificial sweetener, such as saccharin
- lemon or lemon juice
- quinine water

Tongues are also used for tasting, but receptors sensitive to different tastes are not spread all over the tongue. You can see this for yourself by doing an experiment with a friend.

Have your friend rinse his or her mouth with water before you start searching for the receptors sensitive to a salty taste. Similar rinsing should be done before each test to remove any leftover taste.

Prepare a solution of salt by dissolving as much salt as possible in about an ounce of water. Ask your friend to stick out his or her tongue. Dip a cotton swab into the salt water, shake off excess liquid, and use the swab to touch your friend's tongue at the places shown in Figure 8. Ask your friend to raise a hand when the salt can be tasted. Some people will not taste anything until after the test is over. Then, when they close their mouths, they will be aware of a salty taste at some point or points on their tongues. At which of the six places you tested can your friend taste salt?

Repeat the experiment to test for the location of receptors sensitive to sweetness. To do this, make a solution by dissolving an artificial sweetener such as saccharine in a small amount of water. Again use a cotton swab to touch different places on the tongue. Where on the tongue are the taste receptors that respond to sweet-tasting substances?

Next, test for the receptors sensitive to sour by using lemon juice. Where on the tongue are these cells located?

Finally, use quinine water to test for the receptors that respond to bitter-tasting substances. Where on the tongue are these cells located?

Do you find similar results when you test other people? Are older people less taste-sensitive than younger people?

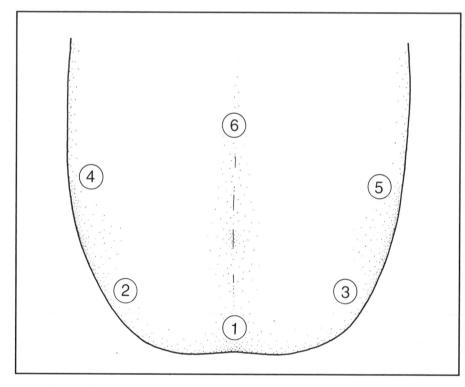

Figure 8: Six places to touch to locate taste receptors on the tongue: 1—front; 2 and 3—front sides; 4 and 5—back sides; 6—back

IS IT TASTE OR SMELL?

You may have noticed that when you have a bad cold, the food you eat seems to have very little taste. Actually, you would know if the medicine you took for a cold had a bitter taste. You would also be able to taste any sugar that was added to, in the words of an old song, "make the medicine go down." What we refer to as taste might better be called flavor—a combination of taste and smell. The next experiment will help you to see how important smell is in recognizing and enjoying various foods.

Ask an adult to cut the apple, potato, onion, and turnip into small pieces. Blindfold a friend who has not seen the fruit and vegetables.

Things you'll need:

- apple
- potato
- onion
- turnip
- toothpicks
- apple juice
- orange juice
- ordinary table (5 percent) vinegar diluted with an equal volume of water
- onion juice
- sugar water
- salt water
- blindfold or large handkerchief
- small paper cups or glasses

Ask your friend to hold his or her nose tightly throughout the experiment. Closing the nose will greatly reduce your friend's sense of smell. Then bring your friend into the "laboratory" and seat him or her near the food. Use a toothpick to place one of the small pieces of food on your friend's tongue. Ask him or her to chew the food and try to identify it. Repeat the experiment with each type of food several times. Record your friend's identifications as well as the actual food being chewed in each case tested.

Have your friend chew the small pieces of food again without holding his or her nose. Can your friend identify the foods better when allowed to use his or her sense of smell as well as taste?

Try the experiment with a number of different people. Are girls better at identifying foods than boys? Do older people do better than children and younger adults? Do you have any reason for believing that some people have a stronger sense of smell than others?

This experiment can also be done by having your friends sip different solutions. This test may be even more puzzling to them since solid foods have different textures that might help people identify them.

Repeat the experiment using the different liquids listed under "things you'll need." Let your friend, while holding his or her nose, take just a sip of each liquid from a small cup or glass. Which liquids do you think he or she might be able to identify even without being able to smell?

Repeat the experiment with each liquid several times. Record your friend's identification as well as the actual liquid being sipped in each case tested. How well did your friend do?

Try the experiment with a number of different people. Are boys better at identifying the liquids than girls? Do older people do better than children and younger adults? Does this experiment give you any reason for believing that some people have a stronger sense of smell than others?

WET TONGUE, DRY TONGUE

Stick out your tongue and wipe it dry with a clean paper towel. Continue to keep your tongue out during this experiment. As shown in Figure 8A, place a few sugar crystals on your dry tongue at the same time you start a stopwatch or note the time on a clock or a watch with a sweep second hand or second mode. How long does it take before you can recognize the sweet taste of the sugar?

Things you'll need:
- paper towels
- sugar
- salt
- sweetened powdered soft drink mix
- clock or watch with second hand or second mode

Rinse your mouth with water before you repeat the experiment. But this time do not dry your tongue before adding about the same number of sugar crystals. How long does it take before you can taste the sugar this time? What do you conclude?

Repeat the experiment with salt crystals in place of the sugar. Repeat it again with the sweetened powdered soft drink mix. Do you reach the same conclusion each time?

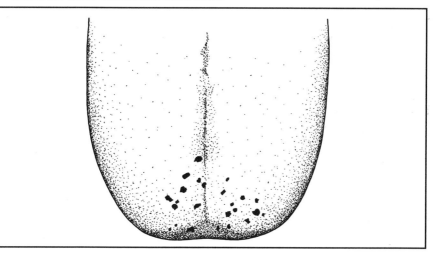

Figure 8A: Sugar crystals on a dry tongue

EARS ARE FOR HEARING

When you speak, your vocal cords vibrate and send pulses of air from your mouth into the air. When these vibrations reach your eardrum (see Figure 9), they cause it to vibrate back and forth. Your eardrum, in turn, causes the three bones in your middle ear to vibrate. These bones transmit the vibration to the coiled cochlea in your inner ear. Inside the cochlea are receptor cells that respond to the vibrations and send nerve impulses to your brain. It is in the brain that you hear sounds and interpret certain combinations as meaningful words.

Things you'll need:

- ruler
- balloon
- metal dining fork
- tape recorder and recording tape
- string
- metal coat hanger or a serving spoon
- blindfold or cloth napkin
- rubber hose, 4 to 5 feet long

Sound and Vibrations

Sound is caused by vibrating objects. The vibrations are carried by the air to your ear. To see how different vibrations sound, hold a ruler against a table top. Let most of the ruler extend beyond the table while you hold the last several inches firmly against the edge of the table. Pluck the free end of the ruler. Does it vibrate? Can you hear a sound? Move the ruler so that less of it extends beyond the edge of the table. Again pluck the end of the ruler. Continue to decrease the length of the ruler that is free to vibrate in small steps. As you do so, what happens to the rate at which the ruler vibrates up and down? What happens to the sound you hear? How is the rate at which the ruler vibrates related to the length that is free to move?

The rate at which the ruler vibrates is called its frequency of vibration. If it vibrates up and down thirty times in one second, its

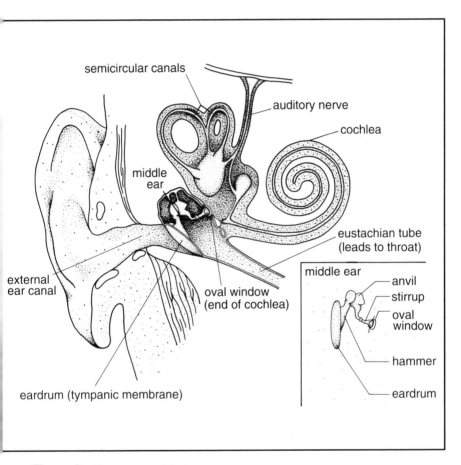

Figure 9: The structure of the human ear

frequency is thirty vibrations per second. If it vibrates one hundred times in two seconds, its frequency is fifty vibrations per second. How is the pitch of the sound you hear coming from the vibrating ruler related to its frequency?

Dogs bark, cats meow, mice squeak, and dolphins click, while humans speak and sing. Most mammals make some kind of sound. In the case of humans, we know that the sounds are used for communicating with one another. Some studies suggest that animals may communicate in this way as well. In any case, it is possible to measure the range of frequencies that various animals can emit and hear. Those frequency ranges are summarized for a few mammals in Table 3.

Which animal listed in the table has the widest range of hearing? Which animal has the widest voice range? Can humans hear any of the sounds made by bats? Can bats hear a dog if it barks at them? Can they hear us if we shout at them?

Perhaps you have a dog whistle that can be used to call your dog without disturbing your neighbors. In fact, you cannot hear the whistle when you blow it. How does such a whistle work?

ANIMAL	RANGE OF VOICE FREQUENCY*	RANGE OF HEARING FREQUENCY*
human	85–1100	20–20,000
dog	450–1080	15–50,000
cat	760–1520	60–65,000
bat	10,000–120,000	1,000–120,000
porpoise	7,000–120,000	150–150,000

Table 3: The frequency range of sounds emitted by various animals and the frequencies that they can hear.

*vibrations per second

Feeling Sound

Put your fingers along the sides of your Adam's apple (larynx) as you sing a note or speak. Can you feel the vibrations?

Hold your hand in front of your mouth as you speak. Can you feel air being forced out of your mouth as you talk?

Blow up a balloon, tie it, and hold it with your fingertips in front of your mouth. Now speak or sing a note. Can you feel the air vibrating inside the balloon?

Sound Through Bone

Even if your ears are plugged with cotton, you can still hear your own voice. This must mean that sound can travel through the bones in your head to reach the middle and inner ears. To see that this is indeed true, pluck the tine of a metal dining fork to set it into vibration. You will barely be able to hear the sound through air. But what do you notice when you place the handle of the fork between your teeth? If you can hear the sound, what else must be conducting sound besides the metal?

Hold the fork handle against the bone behind your ear and pluck the tines again. What do you notice? Does sound travel better through air or through bone?

Listen to your voice on a tape recording. You may not recognize your own voice. Normally, when you hear yourself speak, you hear your words through bone as well as air. It does not sound the same to you as it does to others.

Sound Through String

Will sound travel through string? To find out, tie the center portion of a piece of string to a metal coat hanger or a serving spoon. Hold the two ends of the string in your ears. Be sure the coat hanger is dangling from the string and free to move. Then let it strike the edge of a chair or table. What do you hear? What does it sound like? Does sound travel through string?

Does the sound change if you change the shape of the coat hanger or the size of the spoon?

How can you find out if sound travels through wood? Through the earth?

Where Did That Sound Come From?

Ask a friend to sit in a chair while you apply a blindfold. Now snap your fingers at different places around your friend's head. Each time you do so, ask your friend to point to the place where he or she thinks the sound originates. Do this many times. In some trials, snap your finger at a point that is the same distance from both ears.

How well does your friend do in locating the source of sounds? Which position of the sound is the most difficult one for your friend to locate?

Now have your friend try the same experiment with you as the subject. How well do you do in locating the source of a sound? How well do you do if you plug one ear with cotton?

Ask an adult to help you cut a piece of rubber hose about four to five feet long. A piece of old garden hose is good. Mark the exact center of the hose with a marking pen. Ask your friend to place the ends of the hose against opposite ears. While your friends eyes are closed, scratch at points along the hose with your fingernail. How far must you be from the center of the hose before your friend can tell whether the scratch is coming from the right or the left side?

How well can you discriminate the direction of sound when your friend carries out the same experiment on you?

Sound travels at a speed of about 1,100 feet (340 meters) per second. With this fact in mind, use the results of the experiment you just did to find the smallest difference in time that you can detect in the sounds that reach your ears. That is, suppose an object that emits a sound is slightly to your right. How much sooner must the sound reach your right ear than your left for you to know the object is to your right?

Sound and Darkness

Do you think that being able to see has any effect on your hearing? To find out, have a friend move a ticking watch or clock farther and farther from your ear, but always at the same height. How far does your friend have to move the watch before you can no longer hear the ticking? Are the results the same with both ears?

Repeat the experiment, but this time keep your eyes closed. How far away was the sound this time when you could no longer hear it?

Repeat the experiment once more with a good blindfold over your eyes. Be sure the blindfold does not cover either ear. Try it first with your eyes open under the blindfold. Then again with your eyes closed. Can you hear better in darkness than in light? Does it matter whether your eyes are closed or open? Does the presence of light affect your sense of hearing?

Try these experiments with other people. Are the results similar?

Communicating with Sounds That Are Not Words

Often sounds that are not words still communicate an idea or an awareness. For example, if you hear a teakettle whistling, you may know your mother or father is preparing a cup of tea. The sound of an alarm clock indicates that it is time to get up. The sound of a siren with an increasing pitch tells you that a fire engine, ambulance, or police car is approaching.

Make a list of all the sounds you hear, other than words, that communicate meaning to you.

YOUR BALANCING ACT*

You are seldom conscious of the fact that your muscles are constantly relaxing and contracting in order to keep your body balanced, that is, to keep you from falling. Your sense of balance is another function of your ear and the cerebellum at the base of your brain.

Within the bone structure of your inner ear are three semicircular canals (see Figure 9). These canals, which are arranged at right angles to one another like the back, seat, and arm of a chair, contain fluid, tiny crystals, and nerve cells with hair-like endings. When your head moves in any direction, the fluid in the canal that is oriented along the direction of the motion pushes on the crystals. The crystals, in turn, pull on the nerve endings sending impulses to the cerebellum.

Things you'll need:

- water
- wide, shallow dish
- white paper
- tape
- point source of light—high-intensity lamp or a clear light bulb with a straight filament
- flat eraser
- straight pin
- pen
- blindfold

To see how this works, put some water in a wide, shallow dish. Notice how the water piles up on one side of the dish when you pull it. The same thing happens, on a much smaller scale, inside the semicircular canals when your head moves.

The cerebellum also receives and sends nerve impulses to muscles throughout the body. Impulses that indicate to your cerebellum that your body is falling to the right cause it to send impulses to muscles that straighten your body or pull it to the left.

How Steady Are You?

You are constantly contracting and relaxing muscles to keep your body balanced. You are not aware of these small muscle movements, but they are continually going on. One way to detect them is to throw a shadow on the wall from an object on your head.

First, tape a sheet of white paper on the wall of a room. Then place a small light, one that is nearly a point of light, near the opposite side of the room. For a point source of light, you might use a high-intensity lamp or a clear light bulb with a straight filament. If you use the line filament, turn the bulb so that the end of the filament is used to illuminate your head. The end of the filament is almost a point of light.

Stand about midway between the light and the paper screen. Now place on your head a flat eraser with a straight pin stuck into it. The light will make a shadow of the pin on the paper about twice the size of the pin itself. Have a friend use a pen to mark the shadow of the pin on the paper with a fine line. Stand as steady as you can. For how long can you stand without moving enough to move the shadow off the line? What evidence do you have that your body adjusts to keep you standing erect?

Balance and Light

Do you think your sense of sight has any effect on your ability to maintain your balance? To find out, stand on one foot on a flat floor or sidewalk. Be sure that there are no objects nearby that you might fall on and get hurt. How long can you balance yourself while standing on one foot with your eyes open? How long can you maintain your balance while standing on your other foot?

Repeat the experiment, but this time keep your eyes closed. Does your sense of sight appear to have any influence on your ability to maintain your balance?

Perhaps it is the fact that your eyes are closed rather than lack of vision that affects your balance. To find out, repeat your balancing experiment at night in a dark room. Are you able to keep your balance better with your eyes open even if you cannot see? If you cannot make the room totally dark, use a good blindfold so that you are in total darkness.

Possibly light affects your sense of balance even if you cannot see. How would you go about testing the idea that the presence of light affects your balance even if you cannot see any light?

3

The Eyes Have It

Your eyes enable you to see the world, but your ability to see is not found in your eyes. The receptor cells that respond to light are located on your retinas, which line the inside, rear surface of your eyeballs as shown in Figure 10. These receptor cells send nerve impulses along the optic nerve to your brain. It is the visual center at the back of your brain that makes vision possible. How your brain does this is not thoroughly understood.

In this chapter, you will learn about the structure of your eye and how some parts of the eye are controlled by various stimuli. You will learn how images are made on your retina, how two eyes are often better than one even though one eye is dominant, and how different receptor cells are used for straight ahead and sideways viewing. One type of receptor cell responds only to black and white, the other responds to color—red, green, or blue. But when these color-sensitive cells get tired, they can produce spooky effects; they can make you see colors that are not really there.

LOOK INTO YOUR EYE*

In this project, you will carry out a number of experiments that will help you understand your eyes and how they work. You will begin by looking closely at your own eye. Then you will learn how to change the size of your pupils—the dark circles at the center of your eyes.

By making narrow beams of light, you can find out what happens to light when it passes into your eye. Finally, you will see how images of objects can be formed by using a lens.

Things you'll need:

- mirror
- large straight pin or needle
- sheet of heavy black construction paper
- scissors
- lamp
- large, clear, cylindrical plastic or glass jar
- convex lenses (magnifying glasses) of different thickness (focal length)
- light-colored wall or white cardboard
- camera without film
- index card and pencil

Your Eye in a Mirror

Look closely at your eye in a mirror. Be sure there is plenty of light so you can see clearly. The front of your eye is covered with a curved, transparent layer of tissue called the cornea. In the mirror you may be able to see your own image in the image of your cornea. This is because the cornea is so smooth that it acts like a mirror too. If you have a cat, you can see its cornea more clearly than your own. A cat's iris is set back farther from the cornea than is yours.

Because your cornea is transparent, you can see your colored iris, which is located behind the cornea and in front of the lens. The iris determines the color of your eyes. What color are your eyes?

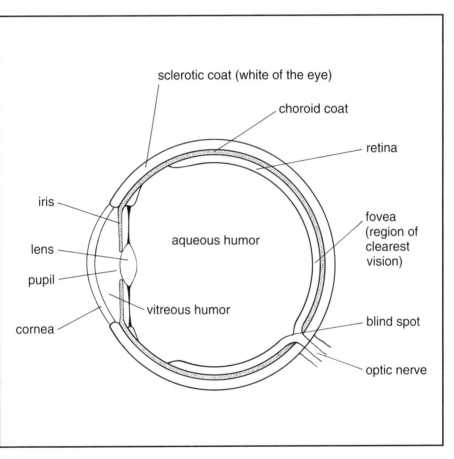

Figure 10: A diagram of the human eye

The black hole at the center of the iris is the pupil. It lets light into the lens. The lens focuses the light to form images on the retina. Although you cannot see beyond the pupil without a special light that doctors use, the space behind the lens and in front of the retina is filled with a clear fluid called the vitreous humor. Another clear fluid, the aqueous humor, lies between the cornea and the lens. These fluids fill the eyeball and give it its spherical shape in the same way that the air in a basketball gives it its shape.

Pupils Come in Pairs

The black pupil near the front and center of each eyeball provides the opening through which light enters the eye. As you have seen, the pupils are surrounded by the colored iris. The iris has muscles at its base that allow it to change the size of the pupil. These muscles are supplied with nerves that respond to the intensity of the light entering your eye. To see that this is true, stand in front of a mirror and open your eyes wide so you can see your pupils clearly. Cover one eye with your hand as you watch the pupil of your open eye. How does it respond to the reduced light in the other eye? Do your iris muscles respond independently or separately to reduced light? What happens when you uncover your eye? Repeat this several times. What can you do to make your pupil shrink? What can you do to make your pupil widen or dilate?

Here is another way to see your pupil react to bright and dim light. Use a large straight pin or needle to make a pinhole about one millimeter in diameter near the center of a thick piece of black paper. Holding the paper with the pinhole close to one eye, turn your eye toward a well-illuminated window. Close your other eye (the one that has no pinhole in front of it). You can see light from the bright scene coming through a circle. Now open the other eye. If you concentrate on the circle, you will see it shrink. If you close the other eye again, you will see the circle widen. By alternately opening and closing your uncovered eye, you can make the circle shrink and widen in a rhythmic manner. How can you explain what you see?

Look through the pinhole once more. This time concentrate on the circle of light. You'll see a number of tiny clear circles with dark circles around them that seem to drift slowly across your field of view. These tiny circles are caused by light passing around tiny particles that float in the fluid inside your eyeball.

Cornea, Lens, Fluids, and Images

When light enters your eye, it is bent (refracted) first by the cornea and the aqueous humor and then by the lens and the vitreous humor. To see how this is done, cut two narrow, vertical slits in the center of the piece of heavy black construction paper. Fold the paper so it will stand upright on a table or the floor as shown in Figure 11. When the light from a single distant lamp in an otherwise dark room shines through the slits, it will form two narrow beams of light.

Place a piece of white paper behind the slits so you can see the narrow beams more clearly. Fill the clear, cylindrical plastic or glass jar with water. The jar of water represents the parts of the eye that refract light. Put the jar of water on the rays as shown in Figure 11. What happens to the light as it passes into and out of the water?

Images Like Those on the Retina

You might consider the beams of light you just made to be "fat" rays of light coming from a point of light represented by the distant light bulb. As you saw, the rays, or beams, were bent by the jar of water so they came together. If the jar of water represents the parts of the eye that refract light (the cornea, lens, and fluids), then the point where they meet would be a point on the retina. It would be the image of the point of light.

To see how such an image can be produced from a real object, you'll need the convex lenses (magnifying glasses) and a sheet of white cardboard or a light-colored wall. Find a room with a window that looks out on a bright and colorful scene. Turn off any lights in the room and stand on the side of the room opposite the window. Hold the lens in front of the light-colored wall or a white cardboard screen. Move the lens back and forth until you get a clear, sharp image of the outdoor scene on the wall or screen. Images like these are formed on the retina of your eye.

What do you notice about the image? Is it right side up or upside down? When you see a tree, do you think the image of the tree is upside down on your retina?

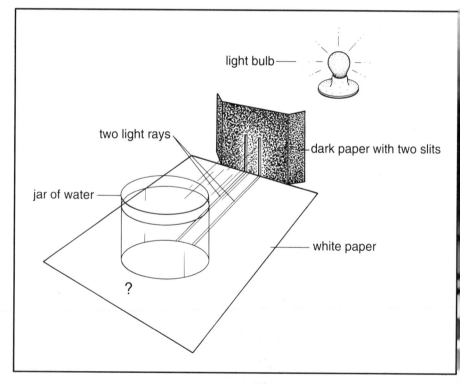

Figure 11: What happens to the light when it enters and leaves the water?

Try using a different lens, one that is more or less thick than the one you used before. How is the distance between lens and image affected by the thickness of the lens?

The lens in your eye can change its shape. When you look at near objects, such as the print on this page, the muscles that control your lens make it rounder (thicker) so it can bend light more. If you look at an object that is far away, your lens becomes less round (thinner). Being able to control the size of your lens allows you to form clear images on your retina of all objects, whether near or far away. You can see a similar effect by using jars of different diameter in the setup shown in Figure 11. What happens to the point where the rays come together if you change the diameter of the jar?

You might also like to investigate the ways that opticians use lenses in spectacles. By choosing the right lenses, people who are nearsighted or farsighted can form clear images on their retinas. As people grow older, the lenses in their eyes become less flexible. As a result, they may need different lenses to form images of near and distant objects. You may have noticed that older people sometimes wear bifocal glasses. The lenses on the lower sides of their glasses are different than those on the upper sides.

If you have a camera, examine it carefully. Then talk to a photographer. In what ways is your eye similar to a camera? In what ways is it different?

The Blind Spot

In the small region where your optic nerve enters your eye and connects with the retina (see Figure 10), there are no receptor cells that respond to light. What do you think will happen if an image forms on that part of your eye?

To find out, use a pencil to make a small, solid, black circle on an index card. Draw a small, dark X about two inches from the circle. Cover one eye and hold the card in front of your other eye. Look directly at the solid circle and slowly move the paper toward and away from your eye. You will find a point where the X disappears. Can you explain why? Can you find a similar blind spot in your other eye?

Viewing the Near and the Far

As you have seen, the lens in your eye can change its shape. When it is very round, it can form sharp images of nearby objects on the retina. When it is thinner, it produces clear images of distant objects on the retina. Can your eyes make sharp images of things that are near and far at the same time?

To find out, hold your thumb about a foot in front of your face and focus your eyes on it. As you focus on your thumb, be aware of distant objects. Are the images of these distant objects clear or fuzzy?

Now, keeping your thumb in front of your face, focus your eyes on some distant object. What happens to the clearness of your thumb's image when you do this? How many images of your thumb do you see? When you focus on your thumb again, how many images of distant objects form on your retina?

When you look at a nearby object, your eyes turn slightly inward so that the images formed by the two eyes fall on corresponding parts of your two retinas (see Figure 12). The brain somehow "fuses" images that fall on corresponding parts of the retinas into a single image. That is why you saw only one image of your thumb when you focused your eyes on it.

In Figure 12, the two eyes are focused on a distant arrow. The two images of the distant arrow fall on the center of each retina. However, the images of the nearby fat arrow fall on different parts of the two retinas—on the left side of the left eye and the right side of the right eye. Can you explain why you saw two images of your thumb when you focused your eyes on distant objects? If you turn your eyes inward to look at a near object, light from a distant object will then fall on

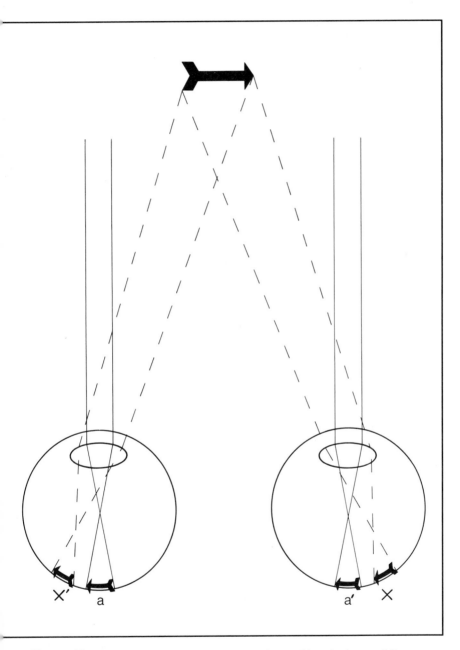

Figure 12: When both eyes are focused on a distant object, its images fall on corresponding parts (a and a′) of the two retinas. However, the images of a near object then fall on different parts (X′ and X) of the two retinas.

different parts of each retina. Now you will see two images of the distant object and a single image of the near object.

You can use what you have learned to entertain yourself and a friend with a bit of science magic. Ask your friend to roll a sheet of paper into a cylinder about an inch in diameter and to hold the tube up to his or her right eye while focusing both eyes on some distant object. As your friend continues to focus on the distant object, have him or her hold the left hand at arm's length and slowly move that hand from left to right, passing in front of the tube. At a certain point, he or she will see what appears to be a hole in his or her left hand. Why does there appear to be a hole in the left hand? What happens to the hole if your friend closes his or her left eye? His or her right eye?

Here's another piece of magic based on the same principle. Hold the tips of your two index fingers against one another about eight inches in front of your face. Focus your eyes on a distant object. You will see what appears to be a small sausage between your finger tips. If you separate your fingertips just a little, you will see that the sausage appears to be suspended in mid-air. Can you explain why?

ONE EYE OR TWO?

Most people can see with both eyes, but they seldom use them equally. In fact, there are times when you can see better if you use just one eye. For example, make a small hole through the center of a card with a pencil point. Bring this book so close to your eyes that the print appears blurred. Now close one eye and hold the small hole in the card in front of your open eye. Can you read the print through the hole?

Roll a sheet of paper into a tube. Look at a distant object with both eyes. Focus on some part of the object. Now hold the tube in front of one eye and again look at the same part of the distant object. Can you see the part more clearly through the tube?

Why do you think the small hole improves your ability to see print that is very close? Why do you think the tube improves your ability to see distant objects?

Things you'll need:

- sharpened pencils
- small card
- sheets of paper
- wiffle or Nerf ball
- scissors
- manila file folder
- tape
- plain-colored tablecloth or wrapping paper
- several brightly colored objects such as thick marking pens

Your Dominant Eye

Most people have a dominant hand; they are either right-handed or left-handed. (The very few people who can use either hand equally well are said to be ambidextrous.) There are a number of ways to tell whether a person is right- or left-handed. You might like to test a few of them with different people. One way is to watch them fold their hands or arms together. Which thumb is on top when a right-handed person folds his or her hands? Which hand is on top when right-handed people cross their arms? Ask them to clasp their hands behind their backs. Which hand clasps the other when the person is right-handed? When the person is left-handed? Or ask them to draw a profile of a face. In which direction is the face turned when a right-handed person does the drawing? When a left-handed person does the drawing? Are you surprised by the results?

Do people also have a dominant eye? To find out, try this experiment. With both eyes open, align your thumb with some distant object. Now close first one eye and then the other. Which eye did you use to align your thumb? Which eye do you think is your dominant eye?

Ask a number of people to try this same experiment. In how many cases is the right eye dominant? For how many was their left eye the dominant eye? Do right-handed people tend to be right-eyed and left-handed people left-eyed?

If asked to read a passage with one eye, do people use their dominant eyes? Do these same people read better with their dominant eyes? Design an experiment to find out.

Judging Distance

Ask a friend to hold a pencil in front of you about waist high. Then, with one eye covered, try to touch the tip of the pencil your friend is holding with the tip of a pencil that you hold. Repeat the experiment with the other eye closed. Finally, do the experiment using both eyes. Were you more accurate using two eyes or one?

Use a pencil to make a dot near the center of a sheet of paper. With one eye closed, try to quickly touch the dot with the tip of the pencil. Try it several times. Then do it again with both eyes open. Was it easier to do with one eye or with two?

Have a friend throw you a wiffle or Nerf ball. Use one hand to try to catch the ball twenty times with one eye closed. Then try it with the other eye closed and, finally, with both eyes open. In which case did you succeed in catching the ball more times?

Use scissors to cut two holes in a manila file folder. Each hole should be about half an inch in diameter, and the holes should be as far apart as the centers of your two eyes. Tape the folder upright to the edge of a table that is covered with a plain-colored tablecloth or a large piece of wrapping paper. Place several brightly colored objects about two feet in front of the folder.

Look through the holes in the folder by placing your head so that one eye is behind one hole and the other eye behind the other hole. Adjust your head until you can see the upper portion of all the objects but not the places where they make contact with the table. Have a friend move the objects several times. Can you tell which object is closest and which is farthest more easily with one or with two eyes?

Look at the objects again through the two openings. Make a sketch of what you can see with your left eye. Then make a sketch of what you can see with your right eye. Finally, make a sketch of what you can see when both eyes are open.

Compare the three sketches you have made. From what you see in the sketches, why do you think it is easier to judge distance with both eyes than with just one eye.

ROD CELLS AND CONE CELLS

Near the center of the retina, directly behind the lens, is a small area called the fovea (see Figure 10). The receptor cells in this area are called cone cells because of

Things you'll need:
- dark room
- penlight

their shape. These cells respond to bright light and to color. They are used when you read or look at the details of an object.

The receptor cells spread out around the edges of the retina are called rod cells. Again, their name comes from their shape. Rod cells respond to dim light, particularly dim red light, but they cannot be used to distinguish one color from another.

The rod cells contain a substance called rhodopsin or visual purple. These cells respond to light by the breakdown (bleaching) of rhodopsin into two smaller molecules. In bright light, most of the rhodopsin is quickly bleached away.

Your Eyes in Darkness

After spending an hour or more in sunlight or in a bright room, go into a dark or dimly lighted room. How well can you see? Sit quietly in the room for a few minutes. Can you see any better now? Do you have any reason for believing that the amount of rhodopsin in the rod cells of your eyes has increased?

After a few minutes in the dark room, try to look at an object. Can you see it best by looking directly at it or by viewing it with the sides of your eyes? Can you distinguish the color of the object? How can you explain these results?

When you are outside at night, look directly at a dim star. Then look at it from the side of your eye. Why do you see it more clearly from the side than from the center of your eye?

A Look at Your Retina

Pigments in the cone cells of the retina are bleached very quickly by light. This means that an image on the retina fades away rapidly if it stays in one place. To avoid this, our eyes are seldom at rest. They are constantly moving in short jerky motions. These motions prevent any one part of the retina from bleaching. Normally, we can't see the tree-like formation of blood vessels, called the Purkinje tree, that lie in front of the retina. These vessels form a pattern on the retina, but the pattern is always in the same place so we don't see it.

If the pattern of this network of blood vessels suddenly falls on a different area of the retina, it will become visible. To make this happen, take a penlight into a dark room. Hold the penlight near the outer corner of your eye as you stare straight ahead. Move the light back and forth a little bit until the blood vessel pattern falls on a different region of the retina. What does the pattern look like? Can you find it in both eyes? Why do you think it fades from view?

Your Eyes as Cameras

To see how light can stimulate receptor cells to create an image on your retina, sit in a totally dark room for at least fifteen minutes. Then ask a friend to lead you out of the dark room into a bright area. Keep your hands over your eyes as you make the transition because bright light coming through your eyelids can cause rhodopsin to break down.

Hold your head very still because you are going to use it as a camera to take a "photograph." You will take your hands away from your eyes for a moment. During that moment, which should not last longer than a second, focus your eyes on the scene before you but do not move them. Then close your eyes again and cover them. Describe the picture you "see" now, having used your retina like the film in a camera. How do the colors in the "photograph" you see with your eyes closed compare with the colors you saw when you opened your eyes to take the photograph? How long does this image on your retina remain? Does it disappear suddenly or does it fade slowly? Does it change in any way with time?

Does the length of time you remain in darkness before taking your eye photograph affect the length of time you retain the "photograph" in your eyes and mind?

Ask other people to carry out the same experiment with their eyes. Do they "see" a similar picture? Do they see the same colors? Does a color-blind person see an image similar to the one you see? Does age or sex affect the nature of the picture taken with the eyes' receptor cells?

MOVIES AND THE EYES

The images that form on your eyes do not disappear immediately. They fade away after about one-fifteenth of a second. For this reason, movies shown at a rate of twenty-four or thirty-two pictures per second appear as a continuous flow of motion, not as a series of still pictures. You can make some simple movies of your own if you take into account the rate at which images fade on the retina.

Things you'll need:

- black tape
- paper towel tube
- 5-inch x 8-inch card
- pencil or paints and brush
- tape
- spring-type clothespin
- wooden dowel or pencil
- set of cards or a small pad of paper

Use black tape to cover all but a narrow slit in one end of a paper towel tube. Close one eye and look through the open end of the tube with the other eye. Turn the tube toward a window. Be sure the narrow slit is aligned horizontally. You'll see just a small part of the window through the slit. Now move the end of the tube with the slit rapidly up and down. Why can you see so much more of the window when you move the tube in this way?

Draw or paint a fish or a bird on one side of a white 5-inch by 8-inch card. On the other side of the card, draw or paint a fish bowl or a bird cage. Tape a spring-type clothespin to the end of a wooden dowel or pencil as shown in Figure 13. Use the clothespin to hold the card at the end of the dowel. Now rotate the card rapidly by turning the dowel between your hands. Depending on what you chose to draw or paint, you will see the fish in the bowl or the bird in the cage.

Because images persist on the retina for a short time, you can make a "movie" of your own using stick figures. Make a series of drawings such

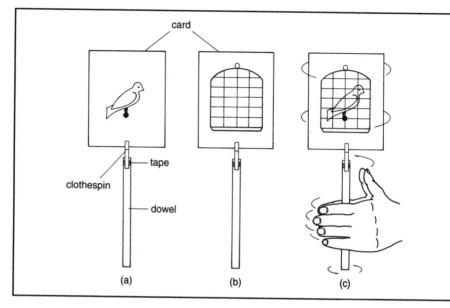

Figure 13: If you rotate the dowel fast enough, you can put the bird in the cage. (a) One side of the card (b) The other side of the card (c) The rotating card

Figure 14: A series of drawings, such as these drawn on separate cards, can be turned into a homemade movie

as those shown in Figure 14 but make each drawing on a separate card or sheet in a pad. When you rapidly flip the pages in the proper sequence, you will see that the stick figure appears to be running. Can you make a movie of a batter hitting a baseball? Of a couple dancing? Of a horse race? Can you make an animated cartoon? What other movie scripts can you draw?

FROM THE CORNERS OF YOUR EYES*

You may have heard someone say about a certain professional basketball player, "He must have eyes in the back of his head!" Good basketball players must have excellent peripheral vision. That is, they must be able to see things that are taking place at their sides as well as in front of them. They must be able to see a player who is open for a pass

Things you'll need:

- ruler
- cardboard
- scissors or knife
- protractor
- nail
- small white cards
- colored pens or pencils

or see a ball coming to them from a teammate to their right or left.

In this experiment, you will test different people to see how good their peripheral vision is. You will measure at what angle, from front and center, they can first see an object, at what angle they can see color, and at what angle they can read letters.

Ask an adult to help you cut a circle from a large sheet of cardboard like the one shown in Figure 15. It should have a radius of about fifteen inches. Use a large protractor to mark angles at ten degree intervals. Your subject will place his or her chin at point X and cover one eye. He or she will keep the uncovered eye focused on a nail straight ahead at 0°. Then, starting from behind the person's head, you will slowly move one of several small white cards along the edge of the circle.

To prepare a card, draw a colored letter about an inch high at the front edge of the card. Use different colors and letters. Can you use the same card for both eyes?

Tell the subject to continue looking at the nail while you move the card along the edge of the circle. Ask the subject to tell you when he or she can (1) first see the card, (2) first identify the color of the letter, and (3) first read the letter.

What is the largest angle at which a subject could see the card? Identify the color? Read the letter? Did the peripheral vision of your subjects differ very much? Does peripheral vision appear to be related to age? Do girls or women seem to have better peripheral vision than boys or men?

Did you test any color-blind people? If so, what did you find?

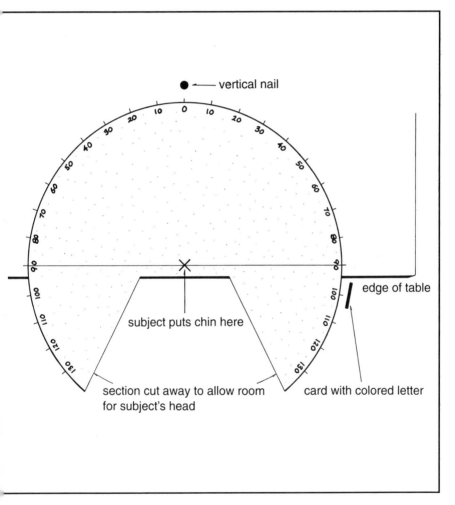

Figure 15: Overhead view of a device for measuring peripheral vision

COMPLEMENTARY COLORS FROM THE CENTERS OF YOUR EYES

If you have ever looked at bright light, you know that even after you turn your head, close your eyes, or turn off the light you continue to see color. The lingering color is called an afterimage.

To study afterimages, cut two-inch squares from sheets of red, green, blue, and black construction paper. Place one of the squares on a blank sheet of white paper. Stare at the colored square for about thirty seconds. Then shift your eyes and stare at a blank piece of white paper. What is the color of the afterimage you see?

Things you'll need:
- scissors
- red, green, blue, and black construction paper
- white paper
- colored pencils or pens
- red, green, and blue light bulbs
- three lamps or light sockets

Repeat the experiment with each of the other three squares. What color are the afterimages of these squares?

Try the experiment with each of the squares again. As you stare at each of them, what do you notice at the edges of the squares?

Suppose you place a small red square on a larger blue square. If you stare at these squares for thirty seconds, what do you think the afterimage will look like? Try it. Were you right? What kind of an afterimage might you expect if you were to stare at a small red square on a larger green square? A small blue square on a larger green square?

Using colored pencils or pens, see if you can draw a picture of a flag that will have the United States' flag as its afterimage. Test it. Were you successful?

According to one theory of afterimages, there are three types of cone cells in our eyes, one for each of the primary colors of light—red, green, and blue. If blue light strikes our eyes, it is mostly the cone cells that respond to blue light that are stimulated. These cells become fatigued through use so when we look at something white, which is made up of all the colors of light, it is primarily the red and green cone cells that are stimulated. Because we see the combination of red and green light as yellow, the afterimage appears to be yellow. Yellow is said to be the complementary color of blue. It is the combination of all the colors except blue. Similar arguments can be made for the green and red cone cells. What are the complementary colors of red and green?

You can check to see if colored lights mix as the theory suggests by using red, green, and blue light bulbs. You can buy these bulbs in most supermarkets or hardware stores. Each bulb should be in a separate socket or lamp.

Take the colored lights into a dark room that has a white wall. Let light from the green and red bulbs shine on the same part of the wall. (Because one bulb may emit more light than the other, you may have to move one closer to the wall than the other.) Does the combination of red and green light give a color that we see as yellow as the theory suggests? What color do you get when you mix red and blue light? Blue and green light? Can you obtain white by mixing all three colors of light?

4

Getting Under People's Skin

The human body is in some ways like a big, complicated machine. It has a frame—the bones that make up the skeleton; a number of small machines—the muscles that move the frame; a fuel processing device—the digestive system, which changes food into substances that can be used for energy within the body; a fuel pump—the heart, which circulates the digested food dissolved in the blood to all the parts of the body through arteries and veins (fuel lines); an exhaust system—the lungs, kidneys, and intestines, which remove burned fuel from the body by extracting wastes dissolved in the blood; and a computer that controls all the operations that go on within the machine—the brain and nervous system.

With the miracles of modern surgery, we can even remove old parts and replace them with parts taken from other humans. Hearts, livers, kidneys, and even lungs can often be replaced if damaged.

Of course, our bodies are also different than machines in many ways. Like most living things, and unlike machines, we frequently can repair ourselves if injured. We can grow, reproduce, and adapt to changes in our environment. Unfortunately, like many other living things, the processes that make us work cannot be restarted once they stop for good. Death is final. But what distinguishes us most from machines is our awareness of the world around us, our ability to react rationally and consciously to the environment, and our capacity to think with foresight and to perceive purpose in our actions and beauty in what we sense and do.

In this chapter, you will learn about the skeleton, which is the framework of the human body. You will learn how joints between bones enable us to bend this framework and thereby move freely. You will find out too how muscles can make the framework move, and much much more.

THE FRAMEWORK*

The human skeleton is shown in Figure 16. You may have seen a skeleton or skeleton model at your school or in a museum. You may even have built a miniature, plastic skeleton from one of the kits that are available. In any case, you will find Figure 16 helpful as you find out more about the human skeleton—the framework on which your body is built. You can do this by feeling along your own bones, which lie beneath your skin and muscles. For parts that are difficult to reach, such as the backbone and shoulder blades, you might work with a friend.

You can begin with the arm. The sharp part of the elbow is the end of the ulna, one of the two bones in your lower arm. Use the fingers of one hand to feel along the ulna toward your hand. You'll find the bone ends in a rounded protuberance at the outside of your wrist, several inches up from the knuckle of your little finger.

On the other side of your wrist, you'll find the lower end of the radius, the second bone in your lower arm. Follow this bone upward toward the elbow. You can find the expanded end of the lower part of your upper arm bone, the humerus, just behind and at the end of the ulna. Can you feel how these three bones come together to form a joint (a place where bones meet)? At many joints, the bones can move relative to one another. Your elbow, for example, acts like a hinge because your lower arm can swing up and down like a trap door.

Your four fingers each contain three bones (phalanges) with a joint at the end of each one. The thumb has only two phalanges. Can you locate all these bones? How can you tell where the joints are located?

Behind and joining your phalanges are the bones of your hand or palm—the five metacarpals, which you can feel best from the back of your hand. Between the metacarpals and the radius and ulna are the eight small bones of the wrist—the carpals. Can you feel any of them?

The bones of your feet are similar. However, the phalanges are shorter and the foot bones (metatarsals) are longer. The ankle consists of seven bones—the tarsals.

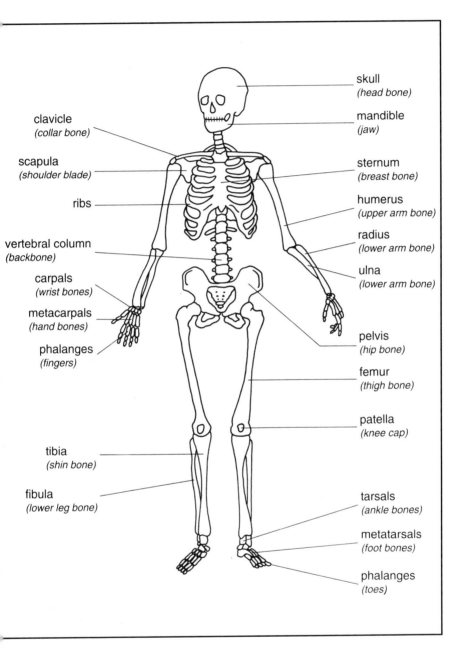

Figure 16: A diagram of the human skeleton

Now can you find the two bones in the lower leg—the tibia, which has a rounded end on the inside of your ankle, and the smaller fibula, which has a rounded end on the outside of your ankle?

The upper leg, or femur, may have a lot of muscle around it, but you can probably locate the lower end of it. It forms the upper side of your knee joint. Can you find the patella, or knee cap?

The upper end of the femur has a rounded ball-like structure that fits into a socket-like depression on the lower outside region of the pelvis, or hip bones. This joint is deep beneath flesh, so you cannot feel it. However, you can feel the upper ends of the pelvis. They lie along the sides of your body about waist high.

Can you feel all twelve pairs of ribs? All but the lower two pairs (the free ribs) are connected by cartilage to the breastbone, or sternum. Despite what you may have heard, men and women have the same number of ribs. At the top of the sternum, you can feel the collar bone (clavicle), which runs between the sternum and the shoulder blade (scapula).

The skull, or head bone, is actually made of twenty-nine bones, many of which fuse together as you grow older. The mandible, or jaw bone, is easy to find because it moves up and down as well as slightly sideways when you chew or talk.

The skull rests on the top of the backbone, or vertebral column, which consists of twenty-six bones. You may be able to feel some of the seven cervical vertebrae in the neck, the twelve thoracic vertebrae that connect to back ends of each pair of ribs, the five lumbar vertebrae of the lower back, the five fused vertebrae of the sacrum, which are joined to the bones of the pelvis, and the three to five rudimentary vertebrae of the coccyx, or tail bone, which lies at the end of the spine.

The spinal cord, which is the main pathway for nerve cells that connect the brain with the rest of the body, runs through an opening that extends through the vertebrae from the base of the brain to the pelvis. The major nerves of the body exit from the spinal cord through openings in the vertebrae.

JOINTS AND MUSCLES*

Unlike the rigid frame of a building, the human skeleton has amazing flexibility. This flexibility is possible because of the joints between bones, which allow our bones to move. Muscles provide the forces that make them move. To see how important joints are to even simple, normal movements, try this. Have a friend watch you try to walk without bending any joints; that is, without bending your knees,

Things you'll need:

- mirror
- spring-type bathroom scale
- straight-backed chair
- plastic cup
- water
- straw
- plastic cup
- flexible straw

ankles, elbows, wrists, hands, or any other joints that act like a hinge. Your friend is to watch carefully to be sure you don't bend any of your joints. How do you feel as you try to walk this way?

Now you watch while your friend tries to walk in this manner. What does your friend's unbending-joint-walk look like to you?

Suppose you try to walk without *any* joint movement. Impossible, isn't it! If you cannot move the ball and socket joint where your femur joins your pelvis, you cannot move your leg forward or backward. You can see why many older people decide to undergo an operation to replace a hip joint that has deteriorated. An artificial ball and socket joint can restore their ability to move their leg freely.

Muscles and Movement

Joints are necessary for bones to move, but the bones move only because they are attached to muscles. Figure 17 shows you how tendons attach a muscle to bone. Watch what happens when you "make a muscle" by contracting your biceps—the muscle in your upper arm. What bones move when you do this?

If you place the fingers of your left hand on the *front* side of your right elbow as you contract your right biceps, you can feel the tendon that connects your biceps to the lower arm (see Figure 18). Can you feel the location where the tendon connects with the bone?

Just above your heel, you can feel the large and well-known Achilles' tendon. Put your hand on this tendon and feel it stretch as you turn your foot upward by contracting the muscles on your shin. What happens when you contract your calf muscle at the back of your lower leg?

There are 656 skeletal muscles in your body. Many of them are located in your face. Here's one way to see the great variety of movements that muscles can produce. Stand in front of a mirror and use your facial muscles to express as many emotions as possible—joy, fear, anger, grief, and so forth.

The muscles of your tongue also allow a great variety of movements—movements that you normally do not think about. Watch your tongue in a mirror and feel its movements in your mouth as you slowly speak a number of different words. When does your tongue touch your teeth? Where is your tongue when you start to say "the"? When you start to say "teeth"? When does your tongue widen? Thicken? Curl? Where is your tongue when you make vowel (a, e, i, o, u) sounds? When you make various consonant sounds?

Muscle Pairs

Generally, muscles come in pairs. Since muscles exert forces only when they contract, one muscle contracts to bend (flex) a joint; the other contracts to straighten (extend) the joint. Usually, in a muscle pair, one muscle is stronger than the other.

With a spring-type bathroom scale, you can compare the strengths of a few muscle pairs. For example, to compare the strengths of the muscles that enable you to kick forward and backward, sit on a chair facing a wall. Place the scale upright against the wall. How hard can

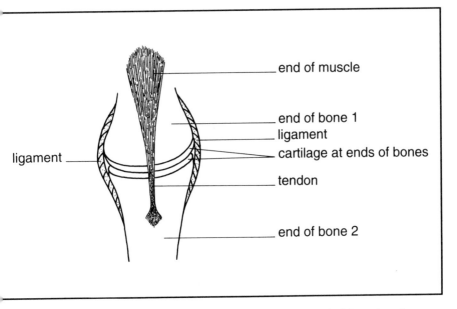

Figure 17: Bones are held together by ligaments that go across the joints where the bones connect. Muscles are attached to bones by tendons. When a muscle contracts, its tendon pulls on a bone. The ends of bones are protected by a layer of cartilage.

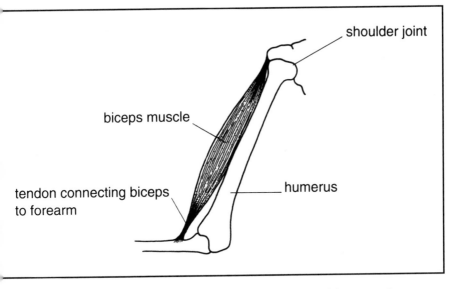

Figure 18: When the biceps muscle contracts, its tendon, which is connected near the upper end of the forearm, causes the bone to move

you push your foot forward against the scale? Now place the scale between your leg and the leg of the chair. How hard can you push backward with your heel?

Figure out ways to place the scale so you can compare the strengths of various muscle pairs. How does the strength of the biceps muscle that bends your arm compare with the triceps muscle that straightens your arm?

Compare the strengths of the muscles in the pairs used to (1) turn your toes upward or downward; (2) squeeze your fingers into a fist or open them; (3) move your head forward or backward; (4) move your upper arm forward or backward; (5) bend or straighten your leg at the knee.

Tired Muscles

Hold the bathroom scale you used in the previous experiment in your hands. Squeeze the scale as tightly as you can. What is the maximum force with which you can squeeze the scale with your hands?

Now close and open your hands to make and open fists as fast as you can for a minute or until you cannot do it anymore. Then squeeze the scale again. How strong are your hands now? How can you explain the difference in hand strength?

Repeated use of a muscle affects its short-term strength. Does it also affect your ability to control it? Design an experiment to find out.

Involuntary Muscles

The muscles we use to throw a ball, run a race, or draw a picture are called voluntary muscles. We can make them contract when we want to. However, not all our muscles can be controlled voluntarily. Some muscles, known as involuntary, or smooth, muscles, are controlled by nerve impulses that we are not conscious of. For example, you have seen that the iris of your eye contracts or relaxes in response to the amount of light that strikes your eyes. Your blood vessels and digestive tract are controlled by involuntary muscles as well.

The automatic control of involuntary muscles by our nervous system enables us to respond to changes both inside and outside our body without having to think about it. After you eat a meal, smooth muscles around your stomach and intestine automatically move the food along the digestive tract. Except for an occasional gurgling sound, you are not aware of all the churning that is going on there. At the same time, the smooth muscles in the arteries leading to your intestine expand these vessels so more blood is available to absorb the food that is being digested. If you are using muscles in heavy exercise, the blood vessels to these voluntary muscles automatically carry more blood to them.

After you swallow food, you cannot control the muscles in your esophagus that carry the food to your stomach. But are those smooth muscles strong enough to overcome the forces of gravity? You can find out by trying to drink water with your head below your stomach. Place a water-filled plastic cup on the floor. Put your stomach on the seat of a chair beside the cup. Then lean your head down and use a straw to see if you can drink water from the glass. Are the smooth muscles of your esophagus strong enough to overcome the force of gravity pulling downward on water in your body?

Do you think you could drink while standing on your head? To find out, *ask a parent to help you.* Put your head on a pillow beside a wall. Have your parent support your legs so that you can stand on your head against the wall. Then see if you can drink water from a plastic cup through a flexible straw.

After doing these experiments, explain to someone how astronauts are able to drink water while "weightless" in a spaceship where objects do not fall but simply "float" about in the ship. Why couldn't these astronauts drink water from an ordinary glass?

The Human Hand

Did you know that the muscles that control your fingers and hands are located in your forearms? To see that this is true, put your left hand around your right forearm. Then turn the fingers of your right hand downward as far as you can. Where are the muscles that bend your fingers downward? Now bend your fingers upward as far as they will go. Where are the muscles that make your fingers bend this way?

Move your fingers up and down as you watch the back of your hand. You can see the tendons that connect the muscles in your forearm to your fingers moving beneath the skin.

A few exercises will convince you that your flexible hand is a very important part of your body. Look first at your thumb. It is opposable to every finger. That means you can touch it to each of your four fingers, and you can use it to hold something with any finger. Your thumb and finger can not only hold and operate tweezers, they can serve as tweezers. Your hands have many uses. You can use them as hooks to carry suitcases or pails; as power tools to squeeze an orange or make a meatball; or as a precision tool to thread a needle or write a sentence with a pencil. You can also use your hands or fists as hammers, scoops, and signalling devices. Make a list of all the ways you use your hand, thumb, and fingers. It will help you realize how useful, flexible, and important they are.

Another way to appreciate the importance of an opposable thumb is to have someone tape your thumbs to your palms. Then try to do some of the things you do every day—throw a ball, make a phone call, write a list of things to do, pick up a book, tie your shoes, eat a meal, and so on. How long does it take before you want the tape removed?

GOING BENEATH THE SKIN

If you have patience and want to see what real muscles, tendons, ligaments, and bones look like, buy a fresh chicken leg or wing from a market. Put the chicken part on some newspapers. *Ask an adult to help you cut it apart* so you can see

Things you'll need:

- chicken leg or wing
- tweezers
- scissors
- paper towels

the different tissues for yourself. The adult will need good tools, and you'll need a pair of tweezers and scissors to pull and cut tissue, as well as paper towels to wipe your hands.

You can probably pull away most of the skin with your hands. Notice and feel the layer of fat that lies just beneath the skin. If the feet are still attached to the leg, you can cut around the lower leg and find the long, white, fibrous tendons that connect to the toes. What happens when you pull on one of these tendons?

The flesh beneath the skin and fatty layer is mostly muscle. Notice how the muscles are covered by a very thin transparent membrane. Try to separate one of the larger muscles and trace its ends. Can you find the tough, white, fibrous tendons that connect the muscle to bone?

Once you have found some tendons, ask the adult to cut away the muscles. See if you can find the wide, tough, white ligaments that connect one bone to another across a joint. If the ligaments are cut through, you can see the joint where the bones come together. Notice the layer of smooth, shiny, white cartilage that covers the ends of the bones. The cartilage cushions and protects the bones. (Human athletes often tear part of the cartilage in the knee joint.) Can you find pads of yellow fat within the joint?

Finally, ask the adult to cut away all the tissue along the bones. You can probably break one of the bones in half because chicken bones are thin. What do you find inside the bones?

Set the bones aside in a warm, safe place until they are dry. You will use them in the next experiment.

THEM DRY BONES

Place one of the dry bones in a jar of vinegar. Cover the jar and leave another dry bone beside the jar. Vinegar is an acid. It will slowly dissolve the minerals in the bone. After several days, remove the bone from the jar. How does its flexibility compare with that of the dry bone you left beside the jar?

Things you'll need:
- dry chicken bones (legs or wings)
- vinegar
- glass jar

The soft, flexible, plastic-like material that remains after the minerals have been removed would eventually decay if buried in soil. Under proper conditions, the mineral or hard part of the bone might be preserved and form a fossil.

Recently an early native-American settlement estimated to be about 9,000 years old was discovered on Cape Cod where the soil is very acidic. A large number of stone and carbon artifacts were excavated by archaeologists who worked at the site, but not a single fossilized bone was found. Why do you think there were no fossil bones at the site?

THE SHRINK TEST*

You may have heard that people shrink as they grow older. This is true of many old people. But have you heard of people shrinking during the course of a day? Could

Things you'll need:
- standard device for measuring height or carpenter's level and pencil

weight and tired muscles cause the bones in the joints of your vertebrae, hips, and knees to move closer together?

To find out, ask a friend or parent to measure your height early in the morning, at midday, and in the evening. The measurements should all be made in the same place with you in your stocking feet. If you do not have a standard device for measuring height, have your friend or parent use a carpenter's level. By placing the level on your head, he or she can be sure that the line made at the bottom of the instrument is level with the top of your head. You, in turn, can measure your friend's or parent's height in the same way.

Do you find any evidence for believing that people shrink or grow significantly during the course of a day? If you do, try the experiment on a large number of people. Does the change in height appear to be related to a person's age? Height? Weight? The time that he or she stands each day?

Teeth Are for Eating

Although teeth are hard like bone, they are not classified as bones. They contain different material than bone, and they originate from different tissue. As you well know, your first set of twenty teeth, which are usually present by two years of age, begin to fall out at about the age of seven. They are replaced by a set of thirty-two teeth, which are usually all in place by age twenty-one.

Ask a young child, possibly a younger brother or sister, if you may examine his or her teeth. Be sure to ask permission of the child's parent too. Look at Figure 19. Can you find the child's incisors? Canines? Molars?

Now ask an adult for permission to look at his or her teeth. Can you find the eight incisors? The four canines? The eight premolars? The twelve molars?

In addition to the difference in the number, what else is different about the teeth of adults and children?

To see how we use all these different teeth, try eating some different foods. Eat slowly and think about which teeth you are using as you bite and chew. Which teeth do you use to bite your food? How well can you chew food using only your front teeth (incisors)? Which teeth do you use to eat celery and carrots? To eat bananas? Lettuce? Nuts? Meat? Bread?

Cows eat lots of grass. What kind of teeth do you think they use the most? Lions are flesh-eaters. What kind of teeth do you think they use the most. How about rats and other gnawing animals?

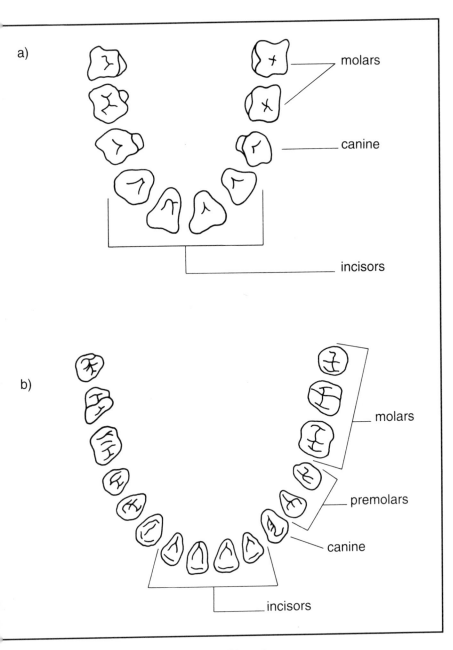

Figure 19: a) A child's teeth (b) An adult's teeth

5

More Projects with People

There are thousands more projects that can be done with people; we have selected some typical ones for this chapter. We begin with a series of projects to examine how we adjust to excess heat and thereby stay cool (or at least do not overheat). You will find, too, a series of projects that examine how fast people grow, not just their height but their hair and fingernails as well. While we are on the subject of fingers, you might like to do a project involving fingerprints. You will find that when it comes to fingerprints all people are truly unique. Finally, we end the book, as you end each day, with a project on sleep.

STAYING COOL*

What can you do to keep your body cool on a hot summer day other than going into an air-conditioned room? One thing you might do is turn on an electric fan and sit in front of it. Does the fan somehow cool the air?

You can find out by using a thermometer. First, measure the temperature of the still air in the room by hanging the thermometer near the center of the room. After a few minutes, read and record the temperature on the thermometer. Then turn on the fan and watch the thermometer. Does the air get cooler?

Since a fan does not cool the air, there must be some other reason why the fan makes you feel cooler. Dip a small piece of cotton cloth in some lukewarm water. Squeeze out the excess water. Then wrap the cloth around the lower end of the thermometer so it covers the bulb of the thermometer. Use a rubber band to keep the cloth in place. When the liquid in the thermometer stops moving, read and record the temperature. Then hang the thermometer in the moving air generated by the fan. What happens to the temperature?

Leave the thermometer in front of the fan until the cloth is dry. What is the temperature when the cloth is thoroughly dry? How does it compare with the temperature of the air in the room when the fan is turned off?

To see what lowers the temperature of the wet cloth, spread a few drops of water on the back of one hand. Leave the other hand dry. Now

Things you'll need:

- electric fan
- thermometer
- small cotton cloth
- rubber bands
- transparent tape
- plastic bag larger than your hand
- aluminum foil
- eyedropper
- water
- rubbing alcohol
- cooking oil
- a dark shirt and a white shirt

hold both hands in the moving air coming from a fan. Which hand feels cooler?

When your hand is dry again, repeat the experiment. Do both hands feel about the same temperature now?

You may have seen a road or sidewalk change from wet to dry after a rainstorm. We say that the water evaporates; that is, it changes from a liquid to a gas. You may also have noticed that the water evaporates faster when a wind is blowing. The same thing happened to the water on your hand when you held it in the air moving away from the fan.

Water, like all substances, is made up of molecules. These tiny particles of matter, which are too small to be seen with a microscope, move faster when they are heated. The molecules in the water on your hand absorbed heat from your body. As they did so, the faster moving ones escaped into the air and were carried away by the wind from the fan, leaving the slower ones behind to absorb more heat from your body.

Normally, when you are hot, you perspire. The sweat absorbs heat from your body as it evaporates. This helps keep your body cool. If the wind is blowing, sweat evaporates faster from your body and you feel even cooler.

A Hand in a Bag

Put one of your hands inside a plastic bag. Use transparent tape to seal the mouth of the bag around your wrist. Then go for a run so you begin to feel hot and start to sweat. Which of your two hands feels warmer? What do you find is collecting on the inside surface of the plastic bag? How can you explain your observation?

Later, when you are cool and resting or reading a book, cover your hand with another plastic bag. Seal it as before and continue to wear it for an hour or so while you read or sit quietly. At the end of this period, carefully examine the bag on your hand. What evidence do you have that water evaporates from your body even when you are at rest?

Evaporating Different Liquids

Lay a piece of aluminum foil flat on a kitchen counter. Place drops of water, rubbing alcohol, and cooking oil side by side, about two inches apart, on the foil. Using your finger spread the drops into parallel streaks on the foil. Watch the three streaks closely. Which one disappears (evaporates) fastest? Which one stays a liquid the longest?

Spread a few drops of water on the back of one hand. Spread an equal amount of rubbing alcohol on the back of the other hand. From what you found out about the streaks of water, alcohol, and cooking oil, which liquid do you think will evaporate faster? Which hand do you think will feel cooler? What can you do to make both hands feel cooler?

People who have a fever are sometimes given an alcohol rub. Have you ever had one? Why are fever patients often given an alcohol rub instead of a water rub?

Dress Cool

Have you ever noticed that people who live in desert climates often wear white clothing Do you think there is a reason why they wear light-colored clothes?

To find out, place a dark shirt and a white shirt side by side in the sun. Put a thermometer inside the white shirt. Look at the thermometer every few minutes until the temperature stops rising. How warm does it get inside the white shirt? Now place the thermometer inside the dark shirt. After a few minutes read the thermometer. How warm is it inside the dark shirt? Does it make sense to wear light-colored clothes in a desert climate?

HOW FAST DO YOU GROW?*

"Growing like a weed" is a phrase that describes almost every person's growth at some period in his or her life. Perhaps you are at that stage right now, or perhaps some of

Things you'll need:

- standard device for measuring height or carpenter's level and pencil

your friends or brothers or sisters are. You will soon find out, if you do this project with a variety of people.

Ask a friend or parent to measure your height once a month for as long as you conduct this project—at least a year—or longer if you find it interesting. Try to space the measurements so they are just about thirty days apart. If you do not have a standard device for measuring height, have your friend or parent use a carpenter's level. By placing

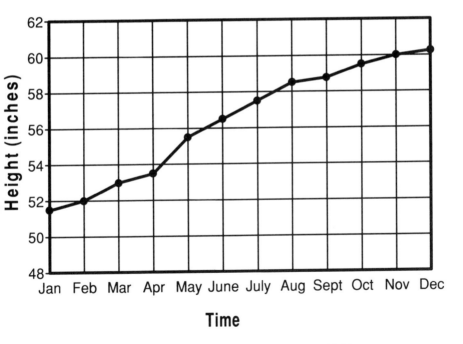

Figure 20: A graph of height vs. time. During which month did this person grow fastest? Slowest?

the level on your head, he or she can be sure that the line made at the bottom of the instrument is level with the top of your head. Take off your shoes before a measurement is made.

You, in turn, can measure the height of a number of people every month. Choose people of different ages. Perhaps teachers at your school will let you measure the heights of several students in each grade on a monthly basis if you do this as a long-term science fair project.

Keep all your data in a notebook. Each year, you can plot a graph like the one shown in Figure 20 for each of your subjects.

The rate at which something grows can be found in the same way that you can measure the speed (rate of travel) of a car. To find the average speed of a car, you divide the distance it traveled by the time it took to go that far. For example, if a car goes one hundred miles in two hours, its average speed is fifty miles per hour (100 miles/2 hours).

How can you tell which of the people you measured is growing fastest? Is the fastest-growing person necessarily the tallest? Does the rate at which these people grow appear to depend on their ages? On their heights? Are the girls you tested growing faster or slower than the boys?

BEFORE YOU CUT YOUR HAIR*

Now that you have learned how to measure your rate of growth, see if you can figure out a way to measure the rate at which your hair grows. It might be easier to work with a friend who will measure your hair. Then you, in turn, can measure his or her hair. How fast does your hair grow?

Things you'll need:
- ruler
- tape measure

You might like to include a number of people in this project. Then you could find out whether girls' hair grows faster than boys' hair. Does blond hair grow faster than brunette hair? Faster than red hair? Is the rate that hair grows related to a person's age? Does hair grow faster if people spend a lot of time out of doors?

How Many Hairs

While you're investigating hair, you might like to estimate the number of hairs on different people's heads. Choose a common particular location on the scalp for each person you test. Lay a ruler along that region of the scalp and count the number of hairs along one centimeter or one-half inch. Then turn the ruler ninety degrees and count the number along the same length again. By multiplying these two numbers, you will have a good estimate of the number of hairs in one square centimeter or one-fourth square inch.

To find the total area of the person's scalp, you can use a tape measure to find the circumference (distance around) of the person's scalp. If you assume the scalp to be half a sphere, then the area of the scalp is equal to the square of its circumference divided by 2 times pi (π). Since π is about 3.14, we have

$$\text{Area} = \frac{(\text{Circumference})^2}{2\,\pi} = \frac{(\text{Circumference})^2}{2 \times 3.14}$$

For example, if the circumference of a person's scalp is 52 cm, then the surface area of his or her scalp is

$$\frac{(52 \text{ cm})^2}{2 \times 3.14} = 430 \text{ cm}^2$$

(If you prefer, you can find the area by covering the person's scalp with a series of paper strips and then adding up the areas of all the strips.)

If, for that person, you counted nine hairs along a centimeter and ten hairs along the other centimeter, you would estimate the number of hairs to be 39,000 hairs because

$$(9 \text{ hairs/cm} \times 10 \text{ hairs/cm}) \times 430 \text{ cm}^2 = 39,000 \text{ hairs}$$

Do blonds have more hairs on their heads than brunettes? Than red-heads? Do girls have more hairs on their heads than boys? Do women have more than men? Do people with coarse hair have more hairs than people with fine hair?

SNIP AND MEASURE*

Every time you cut (or bite) your fingernails, you are reminded of how fast they grow. But how fast do they really grow? With the edge of a fingernail file, scratch a short

Things you'll need:

• nail file
• ruler

straight line across the cuticle at the base of a fingernail just in front of the skin. Measure the distance from the scratch to the edge of the white band at the end of the nail (see Figure 21). Write the measurement and the date you made the measurement in a notebook.

A week later measure the distance from scratch to white band again. Has the scratch moved closer to the band? By subtracting your second measurement from your first, you can find out how much your nail grew in one week. Continue to do this on the same day each week. (You may have to refile the scratch occasionally to keep it visible.)

What is the rate of your fingernail's growth in millimeters or inches per month? Per year? Which is growing faster, your fingernails or your height?

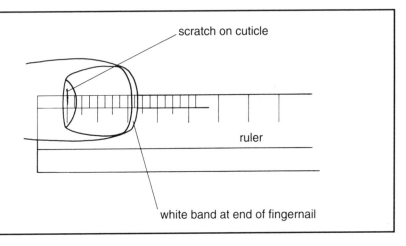

scratch on cuticle

ruler

white band at end of fingernail

Figure 21: How fast do your fingernails grow?

You could extend this experiment into a science-fair project by investigating more questions and including more people. For example, do all your fingernails grow at the same rate? Do they grow at the same rate as your thumbnail? As your toenails?

Ask a number of other people, such as your classmates, friends, siblings, parents, and other adults to contribute data to your project. You can mark their thumbnails so the distance from scratch to white band is the same for all of them, say one centimeter, or half an inch. They may not want to make weekly measurements, but you can ask them to tell you when the scratch reaches the white band. After about two months, remind them occasionally to watch closely and report the grow-out date to you.

A chart like the one below will help you keep a record of all the data.

THUMBNAIL GROWTH TIMES					
Name	Age	Sex	Start Date	End Date	Time to Grow Out

Once the data is complete, you can begin to answer some of the questions below as well as questions of your own that may arise during the project.

Do female fingernails grow faster than male fingernails? Does the growth rate appear to be related to age? Do the nails of any one age group appear to grow faster than others? Is the growth rate related to a person's level of activity or occupation? Does the rate depend on the season of the year? If it does, how can you test to see if it is related to temperature, hours of daylight, or some other factor?

FINGERPRINTS: THE OTHER SIDE OF YOUR FINGERS*

Your fingerprints are covered with a pattern of ridges that is uniquely your own. No one else in the world has the same pattern. When you touch something, you leave that pattern of ridges—your finger-prints—on the object you touch.

To make a set of your own fin-gerprints, rub the side of a sharpened pencil that has soft lead

Things you'll need:
- pencil with soft lead
- sheet of white paper
- wide, clear tape
- clear glass
- cooking oil
- talcum powder
- dark-colored paper

on a sheet of white paper. In that way you can make a layer of graphite on the paper. Now rub the last or outer part of your right thumb back and forth in the graphite. Ask a friend or parent to lay a wide piece of clear tape across your thumbprint. The tape can then be removed and stuck on a sheet of white paper.

If you repeat the process for each finger of your right hand and then do the same for your left hand, you will have a complete record of your fingerprints as shown in Figure 22. The most common general types of fingerprint patterns are shown in Figure 23. Which of these patterns do you find in your fingerprints? Do all your fingerprints have the same pattern or are some loops, some arches, and some whorls? Do the fingerprints on your left hand match those on your right?

Now make a record of a friend's fingerprints. If possible, make a fingerprint record for a number of other friends. Then you and your friends can gather to test your crime-detecting skills. Place a clean, clear glass on a table before you leave the room. In your absence, one person whose fingerprints have been recorded will pick up the glass and then replace it. To make the task somewhat easier while you are learning this skill, ask the "guilty" person to rub a thin layer of cooking oil on his or her fingers before touching the glass.

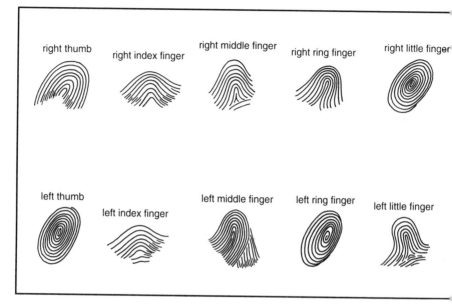

Figure 22: A set of fingerprints

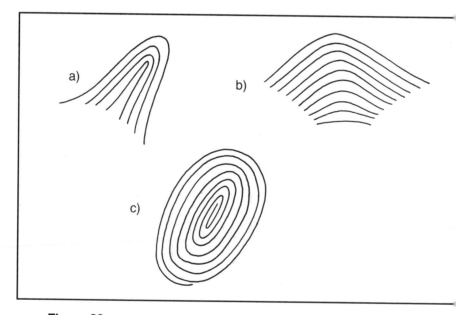

Figure 23: The most common fingerprint patterns: (a) Loops (b) Arches (c) Whorls

When you return, you are to identify the person who picked up the glass from the fingerprints he or she left on the glass. Hold the glass at its base and turn it in good light. If you are lucky, the fingerprints or print may be clear enough so you can easily compare them with the fingerprint records that were prepared earlier. If the prints are faint, you may have to "lift" them from the glass. You can do that by sprinkling some talcum powder on the glass. Blow away the excess powder. Can you see the prints more clearly now? Place a strip of wide, clear tape on the print. This will transfer the fingerprint to the tape. You can then carefully pull away the tape. Placing the tape on a sheet of dark paper may make the print easier to see and identify. Can you identify the "guilty" party?

As your skill in lifting fingerprints improves, you may want to develop additional crime-detecting games or experiments. Perhaps you could arrange a trip to a crime (forensic) laboratory. There you would see how forensic scientists use scientific techniques in solving crimes.

SLEEPY TIMES

How many hours do you sleep each night? Do you sleep longer than your parents? Longer than your brothers, sisters, or friends?

Things you'll need:
- watch or small clock
- a friend who needs little sleep

Make a survey to find out about the sleep habits of different people. Interview a large number of people and ask each of them how many hours they normally sleep each night. For each person, record the number of hours slept, age, sex, and whether he or she sleeps during the day or during the night. If you include babies in your survey, you will need to interview parents or live in the same house as the baby.

Does the amount of time that people sleep appear to be related to age? To sex? To occupation? Do people who sleep during the day and work at night sleep the same amount as people who sleep at night?

Sleepy Animals

You and a friend might like to take turns watching a number of animals to find out how many hours they sleep each day. Do most animals sleep longer than you do? Do you have any evidence that dogs or cats dream?

Scientists who study sleep have placed electric probes over the brains of humans and other animals in order to record brain wave patterns. These experiments show that as mammals sleep they repeat a sleep cycle that consists of four stages as revealed by the brain wave patterns shown in Figure 24.

Examine Table 4. It shows the time that various animals sleep and the length of each four-stage sleep cycle. Does the amount of time an animal sleeps each day appear to depend on its size? What do you notice about the length of the sleep cycles of animals that sleep the least number of hours per day?

Copy the table and add another column in which you list the number of sleep cycles per day. Can you draw any conclusions based on your new column?

ANIMAL	TOTAL HOURS OF SLEEP PER DAY	LENGTH OF CYCLE (MINUTES)
cat	14	26
hamster	14	12
human	8	90
mouse	13	12
opossum	19	23
rabbit	7	42
rat	13	9
squirrel	14	13

Table 4: The total number of hours that various animals sleep each day and the length of each sleep cycle. A sleep cycle is the time for the brain to exhibit the four sleep-wave stages characteristic of sleeping animals.

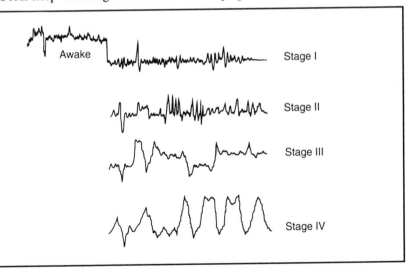

Figure 24: Brain wave patterns during a sleep cycle. From stage I to stage IV, the frequency of the waves (the number of waves per second) decreases, and the size (amplitude) of the waves increases.

Bibliography

Allison, Linda. *Blood and Guts: A Working Guide to Your Own Insides.* Boston: Little, Brown, 1976.

Ayensu, Prof. Edward S., and Whitfield, Dr. Philip (consultant editors). *The Rhythms of Life.* New York: Crown, 1981.

Barnard, Dr. Christiaan. *Junior Body Machine: How the Human Body Works.* New York: Crown, 1983.

Beller, Joel. *So You Want to Do a Science Project.* New York: Arco, 1982.

Bershad, Carol, and Bernick, Deborah. *Bodyworks: The Kids' Guide to Food and Physical Fitness.* New York: Random House, 1979.

Bombaugh, Ruth. *Science Fair Success.* Hillside, N.J., Enslow, 1990.

Burstein, John. *Slim Goodbody.* New York: McGraw-Hill, 1977.

Caselli, Giovanni. *The Human Body and How It Works.* New York: Grosset and Dunlap, 1987.

Joanne Cole. *The Human Body: How We Evolved.* New York: Morrow, 1987.

Dunbar, Robert E. *The Heart and Circulatory System: Projects for Young Scientists.* New York: Watts, 1984.

Gardner, Robert. *Crime Lab 101.* New York: Walker, 1992.

————. *More Ideas for Science Projects*. New York: Watts, 1989.

Loiry, William S. *Winning with Science*. Sarasota, Fla.: Loiry, 1983.

Storrs, Graham. *Understanding the Senses*. Lexington, Mass: Silver Burdett, 1985.

Tocci, Salvatore. *How To Do a Science Fair Project*. New York: Watts, 1986.

Van Deman, Barry A., and McDonald, Ed. *Nuts and Bolts: A Matter of Fact Guide to Science Fair Projects*. Science Man Press, 1980.

Webster, David. *How To Do a Science Project*. New York: Watts, 1974.

Wellnitz, William R. *Science Magic for Kids: 68 Simple and Safe Experiments*. Blue Ridge Summit, Penn: TAB Books, 1990.

Index